THE RACE OF MY LIFE

Born in 1932 in undivided India, Milkha Singh is one of India's most iconic male athletes. All through his professional career, his mantra for success has been regular practice, hard work, self-discipline, dedication and the determination to perform to the best of his abilities. Although he stopped participating in competitive events in the early 1960s, he has dedicated his life to sports.

Milkha Singh has always been a romantic at heart, and he is today a contented husband, a proud father and an indulgent grandfather. *Bhaag Milkha Bhaag*, the Farhan Akhtar starrer which met with great success upon its release in July 2013, is a biographical film that depicts his early life and career.

AN AUTOBIOGRAPHY

MILKHA

THE RACE OF MY LIFE

SINGH

with

Sonia Sanwalka

RUPA

Published by
Rupa Publications India Pvt. Ltd 2013
7/16, Ansari Road, Daryaganj
New Delhi 110002

Sales Centres:

Allahabad Bengaluru Chennai
Hyderabad Jaipur Kathmandu
Kolkata Mumbai

ISBN: 978-81-291-2910-9

Seventh impression 2014

10 9 8 7

Printed at Replika Press Pvt. Ltd, India

Mita de apni hasti ko agar koi martaba chahe,
ki dana khak may mil kar gul-e-gulzar hota hai

Contents

Foreword

The past four years have been the most exciting, traumatic and enlightening years of my life, as it was during this period that the idea of making a movie on Milkha Singh, the iconic athlete, was born, bred and executed.

For some the name 'Milkha Singh' evokes a faint memory from the pages of history. However, what most people will remember is that Milkha Singh, hailed as the Flying Sikh, was the famous 400-metre champion, who infamously lost the ultimate race of his life—the 1960 Rome Olympics.

My journey into his life through the film, *Bhaag Milkha Bhaag*, made me understand how devastating this loss was for him. However, Milkha Singh's extraordinary resilience made him step out of the darkness of failure and find redemption.

But his catharsis was not easy, for Milkha had to face his inner demons and deepest fears to come through as a winner, in life.

Milkha Singh saw it all...a bloody Partition, a lost childhood, homelessness, petty crime, and victories hard won—and easily lost. And yet, even after witnessing so much horror and despondency, his will to live every precious moment of life to the fullest is what legends are made off. His life to me is *satrangi*, a rainbow of many vibrant colours.

For me, Milkha Singh's life paints an intricate image of human trials and tribulations, one which evocatively illustrates that true victory lies in racing with one's troubles, not in running away from them...*aapni mushkilon se bhago nahin, unkey saath daud lagao.*

I think God chose me as a medium to take Milkha Singh's story to the world, in order to remind ourselves that there is a Milkha Singh in each one of us.

For me he was...is...and always will be an inspiration.

Rakeysh Omprakash Mehra
Mumbai
June 2013

Introduction

It is really difficult to be objective when you have a father as decorated as mine. His legendary deeds on the track have inspired a nation, and I surely have benefited the most because of my proximity to him.

By the time I grew up and became aware of things, he was done with his athletics career. That will always be a regret because I have never seen him run in an event. But I have felt his influence as an amazing human being every moment of my life.

Things are an lot easier for kids in our country who want to take up sports as a profession now, but when I was in my teenage years, not many parents would have taken kindly to their child's dream of becoming a professional sportsman. But not my father. I think the greatest gift he has given me, apart from his genes, is not knowing the meaning of the word 'impossible', and his never-say-die attitude, evident in the wonderful support and guidance in helping me chart my own life and career.

He had dreams of me becoming an Indian Administrative Services officer. But when I professed that I wanted to pursue a career in golf, the only thing he told me was that I have to be the very best in the business. I do have to thank my dad for the life that I have. If not for his love of golf after giving up running, I would never have followed him to the Chandigarh Golf Club and subsequently fallen in love with the sport.

I don't think he expects perfection from me. But what he surely insists on is the pursuit of perfection. From very early on, he instilled some life-changing values in me, including total dedication, discipline and determination. Those have helped me achieve whatever I have managed so far in my career.

We have shared a beautiful relationship. I must mention a couple of things about him. Given his involvement with sports, he had a very busy life when we were growing up, but Dad always made sure he had time for my mother and us kids. I think the pain of losing most of his family very early on in his life made him cherish what he had even more. And thanks to him and my mother, we are a very close-knit family.

Also, even though he was a strict disciplinarian, he always treated me like a friend. He has always been there to listen to me, and pass me nuggets of great wisdom that he acquired throughout his life. In fact, I have had the first drink of my life with my father and not with my teenage friends. That was the kind of freedom he gave me.

I am glad that Rupa Publications India are publishing his autobiography. His journey has been truly amazing and I hope it will motivate the readers as much as it has motivated me.

Let me leave you with one thing that my dad always says: you can achieve anything in life. It just depends how desperate you are to achieve it.

Jeev Milkha Singh

May 2013

Prologue

When I reflect upon my life, I can clearly see how my passion for running has dominated my life. The images that flash through my mind are those of me running...running...running...

- sprinting from one shady patch to another to escape the blistering heat of the sun on my journey to school
- fleeing the massacre on that fearsome night when most of my family was slaughtered
- racing trains for fun
- outrunning the police when I was caught stealing in Shahdara
- leaving everyone behind in my first race as an army jawan so that I could get an extra glass of milk

- surging past my competitors in Tokyo when I was declared Asia's Best Athlete
- Running in Pakistan and being hailed as 'The Flying Sikh'

Each of these moments brings back bittersweet memories as they represent the different stages of my life, a life that has been kept afloat by my intense determination to triumph in my chosen vocation.

1

Life in Undivided India

I came into this world on a cold dark night, under a thatched roof, in the small village of Gobindpura, tehsil Kot Addu in Muzzafargarh district, now in Pakistan. Till today, I do not know the exact date or time of my birth. Such details were of little consequence in those days. What mattered most to simple rural communities like ours was the present, not the past or the future, just the ebb and flow of our daily lives. However, as I grew older I realized how necessary it was to have a date of birth and so, for official reasons, it has now been recorded on my passport as 20 November 1932.

We were a large but contented family. My father, Sampuran

Singh, was a small-time farmer, with a piece of land that provided the family with food and the cattle with fodder. My mother, Chawali Kaur, was a simple woman, who was devoted to her husband and children. I can still conjure up memories of her sitting at the chakki, grinding wheat to make rotis to feed us. My brothers, Amir, Daulat and Makhan, and sisters, Makhani, Hoondi and Isher, were older than me, while Gobind was the youngest. Amir, the eldest among us eight siblings, was fifteen years older than me.

In those days children were married off at a very young age, and our family was no different. My father had married off all my three sisters and two of my older brothers. Amir and Daulat lived nearby with their wives and children. Among my sisters, only Makhani lived in Gobindpura. Hoondi's home was in a village some 60 kilometres away, while Isher lived far away in Hyderabad, Sind. Isher was my favourite sister, and I would really look forward to her visits back home, especially since she would always bring me the sweets I loved—it was always a huge treat.

We lived in a basic, two-roomed mud house—one room was shelter for the cattle and storeroom for the fodder, while the other was our living quarters. During the day, my brothers worked in the fields with Father, tilling the land, sowing seeds and harvesting crops. Gobind and I, being the youngest, were allowed to spend the day playing with the other village lads. At dusk, we would return home and the entire family would gather around our mother who would lovingly feed us with piping hot rotis with generous dollops of ghee.

Father, though illiterate himself, was a strong advocate of the benefits of a good education, but money was always a hindrance. He was determined that his sons study so that they could improve their status in life. However, when my older brother Makhan Singh ran away from home to enlist in the army, without completing his schooling, he was deeply disappointed. I was seven or eight years old at the time. This was in the late 1930s, as war clouds were gathering over Europe. I remember coming home from the village school one day and hearing my mother weeping and wailing as if her heart was breaking, and wondered what tragedy had occurred to make her so distressed. It was then that we heard the shattering news. Although my mother had all her other children around her, she could not cope with the news of Makhan's departure.

With Makhan having dashed my father's hopes of educating his sons, I became the focus of Father's ambitions. The school I was going to was in a village nearby, where classes were held out in the open under a tree. Most of my classmates were from neighbouring villages, and we would all sit on mats on the ground around our teacher, Maulvi Ghulam Mohammad, who taught us arithmetic and Urdu. He was a stern man, and at times, when we had not done our homework or were being inattentive, he would rap us on the knuckles with a twig broken from a neem tree; it stung like a whip. I remember the flat wooden takhat (board), that I would carry with me, and the wooden pen that I would dip into a pot of ink to write my lessons in Urdu. I was completely uninterested in studying, and felt that it was something I could do without. All through the school day I would impatiently wait for the moment when the bell would ring, signalling the end of classes. I was a free bird once again and would rush off home to play with my friends.

Makhan's departure had started taking a toll on Mother's health and she cried all the time. Mother feared that Makhan, like other young men, would be conscripted and sent off to fight an unknown enemy and never return. We were all aware that beyond the narrow boundaries of our village, the spreading flames of the Second World War were threatening us all. Those were innocent days, people were superstitious and the wider world frightened them. Scary tales that *ladai lagi hai aur log mare ja rahe* (the war is on and people are dying) had reached us, and no one knew what the fate of these young men would be—would they be killed or just disappear?

She kept pleading with Father to find him and bring him back home. Father, for some reason, was quite reluctant. However, to pacify her, he went to the recruitment centre in Kot Addu, and after many inquiries heard that Makhan was in Madras, a city that was both distant and unfamiliar. Upon hearing this, Mother's cries got louder and stronger. Despite grave reservations, my father boarded a train and set off on a journey to the unknown. When he reached Madras, it took him almost two weeks to locate my brother. He had no idea about where Makhan's unit was or any other details; he could only ask if there were any turbaned (Sikh) soldiers around. He wandered through the city, visiting all the army centres, waiting to catch a glimpse of Makhan. He finally got some leads that led him to Makhan. His patience had paid off. Both father and son had a very emotional reunion, but when my father tried to persuade him to return home, Makhan reassured him, saying, 'Father, don't worry, I am safe and will come home for a holiday after six months, when I have completed my training.'

Father returned to Gobindpura, a happier man, and was able to convince Mother that Makhan was happy in his chosen profession and would be coming home soon for a holiday. Her spirits—and more importantly, health—improved after that, and she waited in eager anticipation for her son's return.

After I had completed Class Five at the village school, my father insisted that I continue my education at a better school. Soon I was enrolled in a government school in Kot Addu, which was about seven miles from Gobindpur. The only other boy from my village to go to the same school was my friend, Sahib Singh. In those days there were no clocks or watches in any home, and it was only when the train to Multan passed by the village that I knew that it was time to start the long walk to school. It would take Sahib Singh and me almost two hours to cover the distance between our homes and school. In winter, it was so bitterly cold that my hands and feet would be numb and frozen with frostbite, and the fog so dense that often I could barely see the footpath. It was even worse in summer, the heat so intense that it felt as if the earth was on fire. I would run as fast as I could from one shady patch to another to escape from the blazing sun, but yet, I couldn't prevent blisters from developing on the soles of my bare feet. Perhaps these were the first races I ran, at a time when I never imagined what my future profession would be.

I studied at my new school for two years. I found it extremely difficult to adjust to the new curriculum, particularly learning English, which was an alien language for me. Both Sahib Singh and I were far behind the other students, which frustrated me and made me hate school even more. But, there was no way I could avoid school—my father's wrath would be too great. I vividly remember the day I bunked classes to go fishing with my friends, but when I returned home at the normal time, my mother warned me, telling me to hide because a friend of my father's had spotted us and told him about it, and he was furious. I was beaten black and blue that evening and vowed never to repeat the same offence.

As a punishment, every evening, my father would make me read to him the English lesson taught that day in school. But what he never realized was that I read out the same passage every evening, which I had memorized. Since he didn't know the language, he assumed that I was doing well in English at school, and felt extremely pleased.

I was fifteen years old by then and very conscious of the ambitions that my father had for me. But his high hopes did not achieve the results he wanted. The approaching holocaust deemed it otherwise. The events of those terrible days, as India was teetering on the brink of Independence from colonial rule, have had a lasting impact on my life, and I will never ever forget the hatred and bloodshed that had transformed men into beasts.

2

Bhaag Milkha, Bhaag

Before Independence, Gobindpur was just like one big happy family, where people would be in and out of each other's homes, sharing a meal or enjoying a good gossip. The population was predominantly Hindu and Sikh, but we were on very cordial terms with the neighbouring Muslim villages. It was a bond that had been developed over the generations. In those days there was little emphasis on caste, creed or religion; it was only the brotherhood of man that mattered. But this easy camaraderie between villages and communities was soon to change.

In an effort to bring about a compromise between the

squabbling political parties, the British had agreed to partition the subcontinent along religious lines, with Muslim-majority regions going to Pakistan and Hindus and Sikhs moving to or remaining in India. In early August 1947, insidious rumours had begun to seep into the collective consciousness of the people of the region and the tension was palpable. We had heard that Hindus and Sikhs were killing Muslims; that Muslims were killing Hindus and Sikhs. What did all this mean? And why was this happening? We were simple village folk and to us the creation of an India and a Pakistan were alien concepts. Our only concerns were to till our lands, earn our daily bread and live in harmony with our neighbours, whether they were Muslim, Hindu or Sikh. How would this break up affect us? We were soon to learn how devastating the consequences were.

The spread of such vicious stories was fast and furious, and soon the rumours became realities as the violence edged closer to Gobindpur and its environs. Our friendly Muslim neighbours had been threatened by the more radical Muslim groups from Rawalpindi and Dera Ghazi Khan, who accused them of supporting and sheltering the murderers of their brothers. They abused them, thundering, *'Haramzadon, kafir ko panah dete ho* (you bastards are giving the unbelievers shelter).'* As a result, the children who would play with us, stayed away, and the bonhomie that we had once shared vanished overnight. People from different communities had begun to look at each other with fear and suspicion. The fear was on both sides and depended on which community dominated where.

I vividly remember the meeting at our village gurudwara

to decide how to face the looming bloodbath. We had received ultimatums from the Muslim rioters demanding that we must cut our hair, circumcise baby boys, eat beef and embrace Islam if we wanted to stay on in Pakistan. These demands were unacceptable; how could we eat beef when we worship cows like our mothers? No, we would rather sacrifice our lives than convert to Islam. Another Sikh village had joined forces with Gobindpur and we were all prepared to fight with all our strength. The women would take refuge in the gurudwara, the men would patrol the boundaries, keeping watch on all four directions, while the boys and young men would be on guard to protect the honour of the women. We had no guns, just dandas, kirpans, talwars and kulhadhis (axes), that were used to cut trees with, but our strongest weapon was our courage and belief that we would rather die than succumb to their threats and abuses.

On 14 August 1947, British India was partitioned into India and Pakistan. Then, at the 'stroke of the midnight hour' on 15 August 1947, India became an independent nation. Almost simultaneously, borders were being drawn along the west and the east that would divide the subcontinent. We found ourselves on the wrong side of the border. Almost overnight, the unrest intensified, plunging the lands along the newly drawn borders into chaos and confusion. Politics had poisoned people's minds and hitherto friendly relationships were destroyed by the sweeping waves of hatred and communalism. People no longer behaved like human beings, they had become animals. Hindus, Sikhs and Muslims were brutally massacred, thousands of homes destroyed, mothers lost their husbands and children. There was only bloodshed everywhere.

Makhan, in the meantime, had got married to Isher's sister-in-law, and he and his regiment, the Army Supply Core (ASC), were posted in Multan, some 100 kilometres from Gobindpura. When he heard the news of the terrible danger our village was in, he was given permission by his commanding officer to go home and rescue his family and friends. Accompanied by a few jawans, he left Multan in an army truck, but when they reached Kot Addu, they found the town in flames and heard the heart-rending cries of afflicted citizens. The widespread rioting horrified them, but there was little they could do to save the Hindus and Sikhs in a town where the Muslims were in a majority. An armed and angry mob surrounded the army truck. But just when Makhan and his fellow jawans were about to retaliate in self-defence, the police arrived and assured Makhan that since they were soldiers, their safety would be guaranteed in the town. They were told to hand over their weapons, so that the mob stopped seeing them as a threat. They also promised that help would be sent to our beleaguered village. Makhan and his fellow jawans were then asked to drive to the police station, but when they reached there, they were thrown into jail. It was at that moment that Makhan realized how shockingly they had been betrayed, and that instead of providing succour, the police had paved the way for the destruction of our village by passing on the details of our village to the marauders.

When Father heard the news that Makhan was in jail, he and my brother Daulat Singh left for Kot Addu at once. At the police station, Makhan urged Father to leave Gobindpur, warning him of the imminent danger the village faced, but Father refused. He stated that he would rather die than abandon his home and land and flee like a coward.

As my brother had warned, catastrophe was awaiting the people of Gobindpur. The policemen at Kot Addu had not only passed on the name and location of our village to the Muslim fanatics, but also equipped them with guns and ammunition and instructed them to obliterate our Sikh village. The following evening after my father returned, hordes of militant fanatics and looters fuelled by the flames of communal hatred, besieged our village, camping just five hundred yards away. We could see the flaming torches they had placed on the ground and hear their angry voices shouting that we must convert at once. Heroically, our lambardar (sarpanch) leapt on to his horse and galloped to the Muslim camp to tell them that we would neither convert nor leave our village and homes. Incensed by his boldness, someone shot him in the back as he was riding back, killing him instantly. We were terrified by what had happened and fervently prayed to our Gurus to give us strength and courage to fight the ferocious mob.

The attack came soon after at about 4 a.m. The hordes, waving guns and talwars, broke through our defences, killing anyone who came in their way. It was a bloody encounter— women hiding in the gurudwara while outside, every man and boy put up a brave fight, in a desperate attempt to ward off the attack, but our lathis were no match for their guns. They were killing everyone in sight. I tried to hide, running from one spot to another to escape being caught. I saw my father fighting valiantly, then I saw him fall, fatally struck by a horse-riding murderer. As he fell, Father screamed 'Bhaag Milkha, bhaag.' I was petrified and could barely move. As the carnage continued, I thought I heard my mother's wails of anguish as our village gurudwara, where she had sought refuge, went up in flames. It was only much later that I found out what had happened to the rest of my family that night; how my brothers, Daulat and Amir, killed their own wives and daughters lest they fell into wrong hands, before they themselves were slaughtered; the deaths of my baby brother, Gobind, and sister, Makhani. My sister, Hoondi, who was in Gobindpur that night, was the only member of my family who escaped. She was outside the burning gurudwara when she heard the terrified cries of her one-year-old daughter who was trapped inside. Fearlessly, she braved the flames, rescued the baby and ran away. Such is a mother's love.

With my father's warning 'Bhaag Milkha, bhaag' running through my head I fled for my life, sometimes running, sometimes walking all the way to Kot Addu. It was one of the most terrifying journeys of my life. In my traumatized state, I imagined that every sound or rustle was that of a lurking assassin waiting to kill me. I was in such a trance and till today, I do not know how I reached the railway station. The blood-smeared train to Multan was standing at the platform and I jumped into the first compartment I saw and hid under the berth. It was reserved for ladies, and soon some burqa-clad women entered. When they saw me they tried to raise a hue and cry, thinking that I was a thief, but I fell at their feet with folded hands, and begged them to save my life by not revealing my presence to the authorities. My pathetic plight evoked their pity and they allowed me to remain in their compartment

Back at Kot Addu, Makhan collapsed when he heard the news about the village's annihilation. During his period of confinement, his commanding officer (CO) in Multan had made repeated telephone calls to the police to free his men. But when he received no response, he arrived in Kot Addu with two trucks filled with soldiers to secure their release and take them to Gobindpura. As Makhan, his CO and the other jawans entered the village, the sight before them was terrible to behold and the stench overpowering. The fields were soaked with blood and decomposing bodies lay scattered around, a feast for vultures and dogs. Identification of the dead was almost impossible, and in desperation, the soldiers placed all the bodies, including those of my family, in one big heap, poured kerosene over them and cremated them. More than fifteen hundred villagers perished on that fateful day in Gobindpura. It had taken just a few hours to annihilate my family, home and native village.

When I reached Multan, I went straight from the station to my brother's quarters in the army barracks. His wife, Jeet, was there and we both waited eagerly for Makhan to return from Kot Addu. It took him about three or four days to get back to Multan. I broke down and wept inconsolably upon seeing him standing at the door. We hugged each other tightly and kept crying for a very long time. Then he gave us the full story about his confinement in jail and the gory massacre in my village. I had lost everything I cared for—it was the end of my childhood.

As the days went by, we heard other terrible accounts about what was happening all around us, and it seemed obvious that we would no longer be safe in Multan. Finally, an official order was circulated stating that the families of all Hindu and Sikh armed forces personnel in what was now Pakistan were to be evacuated to India immediately. The regiments were asked to stay on until further notice. Jeet and I, along with other families, boarded a military truck for a long, eight-hour drive to the Hussainiwala–Ferozepur border. It was a silent journey. We were all displaced people who had lost what had mattered most in our lives, and an uncertain future lay ahead of us. How would we start anew? How would we put down roots in a land we knew so little about? My mind was still numb due to the enormity of the tragedy and I had no clue how to pick up the pieces of my shattered life.

3

Ten Days in Jail

Ferozepur was a sea of refugees, who were desperate to find a familiar face—a husband, wife, child or relative. We were all in the same boat, searching for survivors or finding shelter. After days of aimless loitering, I came upon a dilapidated house abandoned by a Muslim family. Though we had some sort of a roof over our heads, it was almost impossible to find food that would feed the two of us. But the lack of money had made me resourceful. I made frequent forays into the army barracks, where I would polish shoes or do some other menial chores for the soldiers, in exchange for leftover or discarded dal and rotis, which I would take back to share with Jeet. On some days we went to sleep hungry.

We had by now lost all contact with Makhan, who was still in Pakistan with his regiment, but there was little time to worry—we had other, more immediate problems to cope with. At the end of August, the swollen Sutlej river that runs through Ferozepur overflowed its banks and the city was swept by devastating floods. Jeet and I managed to save ourselves by climbing on to the roof of a submerged house, but what little possessions we had with us were washed away. By now I had had enough of Ferozepur and was very keen to leave and move to Delhi, where, I had heard, that it was easy to find jobs. Clinging to one another, we waded through the floodwaters towards the railway station.

Once again, a sea of humanity surrounded us. There was absolute chaos at the station with people moving this way and that with no sense of direction. Getting to Delhi was my priority, but the refugee trains were so overcrowded that it was almost impossible to find a seat. Luckily, Jeet managed to squeeze into the ladies' compartment, but I could only find place on the roof. From my elevated position I could see caravans of men, women and children, some on foot, some on bullock carts, cycles or any mode of transport, moving towards India or Pakistan. It was a heart-rending sight, this mass migration of people who had lost loved ones, homes and belongings in what must be one of the greatest tragedies of history.

Memories of those bloodthirsty events of that August still haunt me. I had lost most of my family, and yet, I recall the kindness of the ladies on the train. Although I bemoaned my lost childhood, I also knew that I had to find the strength and courage to face whatever lay ahead.

Once we reached Old Delhi railway station, we, like thousands of other refugees, were stranded on the platform with no clue of where to go or what to do. We had no money or contacts, so I teamed up with a couple of other boys to try to find work, but we soon discovered that in those unsettled days, people were wary of employing refugees. Finally, I found a cleaning job in a shop at Ajmeri Gate, which would give me a salary of ten rupees. Jeet and I spent a few chaotic days at the station, mingling with the other displaced people; we were always scared about what would become of us, where would we go. I can still remember how desperate people were and the intense hunger that would drive them to grab the free food distributed by charitable trusts—it was like vultures attacking their prey.

When we had arrived, we had registered our names at one of the help desks in the hope that we would find some members of our families. Throughout the day and night, regular announcements were made, giving the names and whereabouts of relatives. It was then that I heard that my sister, Isher, her husband and his family, had survived the holocaust and were living in Shahdara. When we reached their house, the family reunion was tearful and poignant. At last we had found some family members who were alive and a place to stay.

My joy was short-lived, however. I had barely been in that house a few days when I saw how badly Isher was being treated by her in-laws, particularly her mother-in-law, an enormously fat lady, who would sit on a manjee (cot) all day, issuing orders to Isher. Jeet, on the other hand, was treated with great respect; she was the only daughter among seven brothers and her husband was in the army, which was regarded as a steady profession in those days. It hadn't taken her long to forget our recent hardships and the bond we had shared travelling from Multan to Delhi.

My poor sister worked like an unpaid maid in that house, waking up at 4 a.m. to start her chores, which included washing clothes and utensils, cooking the meals, looking after her young brothers-in-law and fulfilling whatever demands her husband's family made on her. At the same time, she was a dutiful wife and would present her husband with a child at regular intervals. It was a large family, in keeping with the times, and my sister had to labour from morning to night to keep them happy, but they were never satisfied, and even if she made the slightest mistake, they would thrash her mercilessly. Their unkindness and ingratitude upset me deeply, but there was little I could do to stop them. I kept hoping Makhan would come back and save his sister.

As the days passed, I soon realized that I was not welcome. Jeet's family constantly taunted and mocked me by saying that I was a useless, good-for-nothing fellow, who could only sit around all day and eat their food; that I should go out and fend for myself rather than being a burden on them. It reached such a point that I was given only one meal a day. I would then remember my mother and how she would feed her husband, children and extended family with what little was available.

I missed her so much that I would sit and cry, indulging in bouts of self-pity at my helplessness. Isher was deeply distressed by my plight and would surreptitiously give me a couple of rotis, whispering, 'Bhaag ja, bhaag, if they find out they will beat me.' These I would eat with salt or an onion, as I was not allowed any dal or vegetables.

By now we had heard that Makhan and his unit were back in India, but we had no idea where he was. The situation at home had made me so unhappy that my health deteriorated. Yet, on some days I reverted to being a carefree lad again—racing trains, flying kites or laughing and cracking jokes with my friends. I would have liked to have resumed my education, but there was no money to pursue that avenue. It was at this time that I had my first infatuation. I was just seventeen and the object of my 'fancy' was the beautiful fifteen-year-old who lived next door. In those days, the mohalla had only one municipality water tap and everyone lined up there to fill their buckets. That's where I first saw her. She was standing behind me and I offered to let her fill her bucket before me.

That day onwards, I tried to help her in small ways, by allowing her to take my place in the queue, or carrying the bucket back to the house. But we were so young and innocent, and there was little else I could think of to further the romance other than waiting to catch a glimpse. We would look at each other when she left for school, or when she went up to her terrace, or when she stepped out of the house on errands. I would talk incessantly about her to my friends. Finally, I decided to pour my heart out and sent her a letter written in Hindi, wrapped in a ball which I threw on to the terrace of her home. To my delight, she reciprocated my feelings. Our romance took wings, but our flight did not last long.

I still vividly remember the day when I had taken her for a walk after school finished. It seemed magical. We lost track of time and she reached home late. Her parents found out about us and were furious. She was thrashed and locked up in a room. She also stopped going to school.

Soon after, her parents got her married off. I was heartbroken.

The following eight or nine months that I spent in limbo were the worst times of my life. It was also a period that I am still deeply ashamed of. As was inevitable, I fell into bad company, and began to gamble. There was no elder or role model to give me advice or direction or to supervise my actions. As a result, my life went rapidly downhill.

My friends and I would indulge in all kind of nefarious activities. We would steal bags of sugar or rice from the goods trains that were standing at Shahdara railway station and sell them at cheaper rates at the local bazaar. But the thefts were soon discovered and reported to the police, who began to keep a close watch at the station. One day they caught us in the act, and though some of the boys were arrested, I ran so fast that I managed to escape the dragnet.

Fate, however, had other plans for me. In 1948, I was travelling by a local train from Shahdara to Delhi without a ticket, a jaunt I had successfully managed several times before. But as luck would have it, this time I was arrested and brought before a magistrate who stipulated that I either pay a jurmana of fifteen rupees or go to jail. I had not a penny, let alone fifteen rupees, and was thus sentenced to three months' rigorous imprisonment. I was deeply humiliated when the constables handcuffed me and threw me in jail. It was only after a couple of days that I managed to send word to Isher. She secretly sold her gold earrings and paid the fine. I was released, after spending ten days in the company of thieves and dacoits. Often, while in jail, I would get so dejected that I seriously thought of becoming a feared dacoit after my stint behind bars.

Nothing had changed in the house in the ten days that I was in jail. Isher was working as hard as she always did, and the newly instituted rewards for her were regular beatings. I was still humiliated by my stint behind bars and would sit around the house moping. Then we heard the news that Makhan had been posted at Delhi's Red Fort. When he came to visit us, I fell upon him in desperation, bombarding him with tales of our troubles, and about how harshly his wife's family treated Isher. Although he was a hen-pecked husband, completely dominated by his wife, he did try to make an effort to ease the situation during the short time he stayed with us in Shahdara. But his military duties prevented him from being in the house all day, and the ill treatment never really stopped. One day, all my pent-up frustration and anger erupted at the sight of Isher being violently abused yet again. I went into Jeet's room, picked up Makhan's gun, which he had forgotten to take with him, brought it out and aimed it at Isher's in-laws. I said menacingly, 'Khabardar, agar meri behen ko phir se haath lagaya to jaan se maar doonga! (If you dare to touch my sister again, I will kill you all).' They looked at me with fear, and I would like to believe that the beatings became less frequent after that incident.

While Makhan was in Delhi he managed to get me admitted in the local school, but it had been more than a year since I had looked at a book and I found it difficult to concentrate on my studies. Regretfully, I must admit, I could not renounce my bad habits and was back on the streets again, in the company of delinquents. When my brother discovered my truancy, he would beat me.

Despite the thrashings Makhan tried hard to find me a vocation, but before a suitable job could materialize, he was transferred to Jhansi and I was back to my bad old ways. Somehow, deep within me, I knew that I wanted to lead a better, more productive life. I yearned to join the army, but it was 1949 and there were thousands of unemployed refugees who had the same ambition. Hopeful young boys like me would throng the recruitment centres, but there were too many of us and too few vacancies to fill.

I was rejected two or three times. At my first attempt at the recruitment centre in Red Fort, I was one of almost five hundred lads who had queued up, waiting for our turn to come. Then, we were asked to stand in line in our shorts, where we were weighed. Thereafter, the medical officer asked me to run a hundred yards, after which I was asked to expand my chest and my chest measurements were taken. A cross was then marked on my chest and I was informed that I was not fit enough to be recruited. At that time my height was 5 feet 9 inches, and my weight 65 kilograms. Dejected but not defeated, I tried again but with the same outcome.

To occupy myself and earn some money, I began to work as an apprentice at a rubber factory, with a salary of fifteen rupees a month. I would hand my wages over to Jeet's parents only to receive in return dry rotis and onions for my morning meal. The poor diet and miserable work conditions ultimately had an impact on my health and I was seriously ill for almost two months.

Makhan was now posted in Kashmir and I gave him an ultimatum that he must get me recruited into the army if he did not want me to give the family a bad name. In November 1952, with my brother's recommendation, I was selected at the army's recruitment camp held in Kashmir. I was overjoyed. The other new recruits and I were taken by military transport to Srinagar and then on to Pathankot. My final destination was the Electrical Mechanical Engineering core (EME) Centre at Secunderabad.

4
My Army Life

I soon discovered how tough and disciplined life in the barracks was and the strict rules and regulations that dictated a new recruit's daily routine. Time governed every minute of our waking hours, and besides our duties out of doors, we had to make our beds, wash our mugs and plates and store them, with all our other possessions, in a tin trunk under our beds. We would rise every morning at 5 a.m., down a mug of piping hot tea and then assemble at the parade ground for the roll call and physical training, where we had to go through a series of complicated exercises. After breakfast, we returned to the ground where we had daily drills on how to march smartly and in tandem with our fellow soldiers. The rest of the morning was spent performing several military duties, including practising shooting at the firing range. What we all dreaded most was 'fatigue duty', which meant the non-military duties we had to do every day like digging trenches, building roads, gardening, peeling potatoes, washing utensils in the mess, polishing senior officers' shoes and other types of manual labour. If a jawan disobeyed orders or was unruly, he was made to do push-ups and front and back rolls. The harsher punishments were running around the grounds carrying a knapsack full of rocks on the back or the threat of being sent to the quarter-guard or army jail.

Our days were long and very tiring and we all looked forward to relaxing in the recreational room to play carom, read or just sit around and chat or listen to the radio. Each night, just before lights out, there was the final roll call for the day to check if all were present and accounted for.

Our salary then was thirty-nine rupees a month, of which it was compulsory to send ten rupees home. The balance went towards paying the dhobi, tailor and canteen charges. What little was left over we spent watching movies.

The training was so rigorous and the regime so strict that often I would despair that I would not be able to cope and wanted to run away. Some lads from my group had done so because they couldn't cope with the rigours. Whenever such thoughts came to my mind I would recall my early hardships, and think: army life may be tough, but it is better than the sufferings I had endured earlier. Then a fortunate incident changed the course of my life.

One Saturday morning, after roll call, there was an announcement that a six-mile race was to be held the next day, and the top ten, out of some five hundred recruits who participated, would be exempted from fatigue duty and would also be given an extra glass of milk every day. This was in January 1953.

That night, my Punjabi friends and I could talk of nothing else but the forthcoming race. Our other competitors would be the unit's recruits from all over India and we had all unanimously decided that we could not let the Bengalis, Biharis or Tamilians defeat us—our izzat would be threatened if that happened. I barely slept that night—I was so excited, but at the same time, apprehensive.

When the day dawned, all of us recruits, wearing our canvas shoes and khaki vests and shorts, reported at the starting line. Filled with a sense of mission, I ran with great gusto and took the lead in the first two or three miles. When I would feel tired I would stop, rest for a while, and start running again when I saw that the other boys were catching up. Luck was on my side that day and I came sixth in the race. At roll call that night, my name was announced before a large gathering of almost three hundred recruits. Friends, and even strangers, wildly applauded and thumped me on my back, screaming, 'Shahbash!' I was overwhelmed with joy by the attention I received—this moment was the starting point of my career as an athlete.

Our instructor was a former runner called Havaldar Gurdev Singh, who had been with the army for about fifteen years.

Although his task was to train new recruits, he was a good runner and continued to participate in races. This time he was there to ensure that the ten of us would run six miles each day, after which we would be given that promised glass of milk. For me this was a treat after all those years of deprivation. Gurdev was a taciturn, no-nonsense kind of man, whose tough exterior hid his softer, gentler side. He would run with us during our training period, prodding us with his danda (stick), shouting abuses: 'Haramzadon bhaago! (run, you bastards!),''gadho, hamari company first aani chahiye! (our regiment must come first, you donkeys!),' if we did not perform according to his expectations. He would use the same stick to hit the ground in anger or frustration if we were being careless, calling us 'dangar di aulad'. But that was his way of motivating and encouraging us. I strongly believe that he was instrumental in motivating me to strive to become a world-class athlete. Even today when I think of his danda and volley of abuses, I respectfully bow my head in tribute to a great teacher.

Six weeks later, the Centre held a cross-country race. In this event, Gurdev came first and I second. Suddenly I became the cynosure of all eyes. I was twenty or twenty-one at that time, but looked much younger. A couple of weeks later, I was asked to take part in the Brigade Meet in which all the units stationed in the twin cities of Hyderabad and Secunderabad were participating. I was very surprised when they asked me to run in the 400-metre event, mainly because I did not know what 400 metres meant, as I had always run six miles. When I asked Gurdev, he said that I would have to run one round of the track that measured 400 metres.

Foolishly, I remarked, 'What, only one chakkar (round)? I can run twenty chakkars!'

Gurdev patiently explained, 'No, you will have to put all your stamina and speed in just one round, not twenty.'

At my first practice run, I took off my canvas shoes and stood there barefoot, in my shorts. Gurdev clapped his hands for me to start—I did, and clocked 63 seconds in my first try. I was eager to run four more rounds. After all, I was used to running six miles every day and considered this quarter mile of little consequence. For days I continued to practise and my time was further reduced to less than a minute.

On the day of the Meet, I noticed that some young men had the word 'INDIA' inscribed on their vests. They were being mobbed by senior officers and their children, and seemed to exude an aura of power and prestige. I could not understand why this was so and when I inquired I was told that they were those athletes who had represented India in international sporting events. That was my Eureka moment, when I made a solemn promise to myself that I would not rest until I, too, found a place in that hallowed world of Indian athletes who had the privilege of displaying our country's name on their blazers and vests.

The Meet opened with much fanfare. Our unit's team was smartly clad in full khaki uniforms—boots, jersey, trousers and vests carrying the name EME; the Sikh soldiers had tied turbans over their joodas (topknots). The military band played stirring martial tunes as all the regiments marched in perfect tandem round the stadium, dipping their colours before the dais where

Brigader S.P. Vohra, our commanding officer, took the salute, and declared the Meet open. We then returned to our tents to change into our sporting kits.

As soon as the call for the 400-metre race was given, we reported at the starting point. I was very apprehensive; this was the first time that I was competing in such an event and that, too, before the eyes of some four thousand spectators. My fellow competitors had all stood first in national events, and here was I, a puny, barefooted village bumpkin surrounded by stalwarts. I had no idea what the procedures were for such events, or what the technicalities were until the race began. And then it all became clear. Numbered lots were first drawn, indicating the lane in which we would run. Then when the starter, who held a gun in his hand, said, 'On your marks,' the participants would place their feet on the starting line and 'get ready'; and when he fired the gun, it was a signal for us to take off. I came fourth in the race, but this was of little consequence when compared with the line-up of stars before me—Sohan Singh of the Sikh Regiment, who was also the national champion in the 400-metre race, came first, and Pritam Singh, one of the privileged few who had represented India, was second.

I was disappointed but not disheartened. My participation in the Brigade Meet gave me the chance to attend the coaching camp in Secunderabad, and also go to Bombay for the Southern Command Meet, where I was given the chance to be a part of the Brigade team for 4x400-metre relay race.

When I returned to Secunderabad it was back to work as usual—parades, other military duties and sitting for examinations, simple language tests that we had to pass if we wanted to be promoted to the next level. Despite the regular routine, my burning desire to succeed as an athlete never dissipated. In the evening, after a day's hard work, I would carry my food back to the barracks and hide it under my bed. While my colleagues relaxed, I was at the grounds practising. I was still unaware of the techniques needed to run a 400-metre race, but followed the rule of thumb—I would run one round at the swiftest speed, rest and then run another one. I would complete five or six rounds every night, then return to my room, bathe and eat my dinner. This was my nightly routine for many months—a clandestine activity no one was aware of.

Then one night, while doing my regular practice rounds, I was spotted by Brigadier S.P. Vohra, who was on his regular after-dinner walk. He stopped me and enquired what I was doing at that hour. I sprang to attention, saluted sharply, and modestly replied that I was practising for the 400-metre race.

'Why are you practising at this hour?' he asked.

'Because I don't have time for practice during the day, sir,' I said.

This seemingly inconsequential encounter led to a series of incidents that I could never have anticipated. The next day, the brigadier spoke to my company commander asking him to exempt me from fatigue duty, so that I had the time to practice. The brigadier also expressed the desire to meet me. As a recruit, however, it continued to be mandatory for me to be present at PT (physical training) and the parade. The company commander told the JCO (Junior Commissioned Officer), who in turn told my 'ustad'.

The next day, I was summoned by my 'ustad', who severely reprimanded me for daring to complain to the brigadier. 'If you had a problem, you should have come to me, not the brigadier,' he said, poking me in the ribs with his stick. This was grossly unfair. I had made no complaint; the brigadier had spotted me and asked why I was practising at that hour. I had merely, and honestly, told him that it was because I did not get enough time during the day. But the furious 'ustad' chose to punish me by making me carry a knapsack full of stones and run up and down for two hours. I did not even realize why I had been penalized so harshly.

Still, the brigadier's order had to be obeyed. But to get to his office I had to move, step-by-step, up the hierarchical ladder, being interviewed and threatened and abused by each officer. It took me almost a week to meet the brigadier, who ordered that I should be groomed as an athlete, given proper facilities and a special diet, and be exempted from fatigue duty.

This incident opened up a whole new world for me, one that offered innumerable opportunities. The armed forces in India have had a long tradition of promoting sporting events and athletes, and if soldiers show potential and are hardworking, they are given incentives to encourage and motivate them to develop as competent professionals.

5

This was Not Sports

The EME Centre's sports meet, held in Secunderabad in December 1954, was the beginning of my rise. I stood first in the 400-metre race, clocking a time of 52 seconds. A month later, at the Brigade Meet, in January 1955, Sohan Singh won the 400-metre race with a timing of 49 seconds, and I was second, clocking 50 seconds.

Sohan Singh saw my success as a threat to his position, and I now began to experience the hostilities and rivalries that ran beneath the façade of sportsmanship. Earlier, I had noticed how resentful established sportspeople were towards newcomers, who they saw as challenges to their positions.

I had always had great respect and admiration for their prowess and commitment, but now, for the first time, saw how competitiveness had warped their attitudes. Sohan Singh stopped talking to me and even refused to allow me to train with him. His uncooperative behaviour pained me, but in no way did it stop me from practising with renewed vigour and resolve. I was truly saddened by their demeanour.

About a couple of weeks after the Brigade Meet, I went to Poona for the Southern Command Sports Meet. For some mysterious reason Sohan Singh withdrew from the 400-metre event, preferring instead to concentrate on the 800-metre race. His decision gave me the chance to come first in the 400-metre race, with a timing of 49.4 seconds. The applause and cheers I received from the spectators greatly boosted my morale and self-confidence, which is very important for any sportsperson.

The next event that I participated in was the Combined Services Meet in Ambala as a member of the Southern Command team. This was a gathering of athletes from the Northern, Eastern, Western and Southern Commands along with teams from the navy and air force. There were several national-level champions, including Joginder Singh, India's champion in the 400-metre event who was representing the Eastern Command. Once again I came second in the race, reaching the winning post just a few yards behind Joginder Singh. With this success I qualified for the National Games to be held in Patiala in 1956.

The national-level games were one of the most important sporting events in the country, and it was a great honour for me to have been selected. As a member of the services' team,

I would be mingling with the best athletes from all over the country, including sportswomen. What made it even more interesting was that running was just one of the events; other sports including basketball, volleyball, hockey and long jump were also part of the games. For me, everything was new, and it seemed strange but wonderful. I felt like a rustic village boy lost in a big fair.

The National Games in Patiala opened with great fanfare. Buntings, banners and flags decorated the Yadavindra Stadium and when the Maharaja of Patiala, Yadavindra Singh, declared the meet open, hundreds of white pigeons and multicoloured balloons were released. In his inaugural speech, the Maharaja urged all athletes, both men and women, to perform to the best of their abilities because the selection for the Indian team for the forthcoming 1956 Australia Olympics would take place here. This announcement unnerved me. Although I yearned to be part of the Indian team, how could I even hope to be selected? I would be competing against India's best runners in the event, and was uncertain on how I would fare.

A couple of days before the opening of the Games, a sharp stone pierced my heel during practice and caused a swelling. I paid no heed to the injury and continued practicing. As a result, the injury turned septic, and I was ordered by the doctors not to run in the final race. But I could not let anything get in the way of my ambitions, regardless of the consequences. It was as if my entire existence depended on running the finals. I ignored medical advice and ran the race. I came fourth, while Alex Silveria from Bombay came first, Joginder Singh, second and

Harjit Singh of Punjab Police came third. My hopes crashed, as I knew that by coming fourth, I had no chance of being chosen for the coaching camp. But again, luck was on my side. The Maharaja had spotted me running barefoot in the race and had enquired who that boy was. My effortless style impressed him and he recommended that I, too, should be selected for the training camp since I showed great promise. My decision to run in the finals was vindicated.

The training camp was held at the Sri Kanteerva Stadium in Bangalore. This three-week period was a great learning experience for me, particularly since I was being trained alongside India's top sprinters and under some of our best coaches, including Rufus and Baldev Singh. It was the first time I was taught how to start a race as well as the technicalities of running a 400-metre race—to accelerate speed in the last 100 metres. We were made to do hill running and sand running to build stamina and we would lift weights to build muscle strength. We ate healthy food and were given regular doses of proteins to compensate for the nutrients we had lost during training. I was a quick learner and practised zealously. My dedication on the track pleased the coaches, who encouraged me with their praise and support. It was at the training camp that I decided to switch to spiked boots—the latest fad in sports footwear—after running barefoot for three years. I made this switch around the time when Roshan Sports, Patiala, had just started manufacturing spiked boots for the first time in India. I had always preferred the freedom of sprinting without the constraints of shoes, and felt that wearing them would hamper my speed. However, once

I got used to them, I was amazed to find how wearing spiked boots could improve my performance.

At the end of the three weeks, a trial race was held, where Joginder Singh, the star of the event, and I were tied for the first place, both clocking 48.2 seconds. As a result, the boy who came second was relegated to the third place and the one who came third to the fourth. Suddenly, I had become the hottest topic of conversation in India's sports fraternity.

Those of us who had attended the Bangalore camp were in Patiala once again for the final selection of the Indian athletic team. Once again, some of my colleagues reacted in a negative fashion, and I was constantly subjected to snide remarks, but I chose to ignore their jibes. I did not allow their animosity to come in the way of my aim and kept practising hard. However, I was completely unprepared for the sinister incident that almost broke my legs.

The night before the selection race, I was suddenly jolted out of a deep slumber by a hard hit on my legs. A bunch of people had pinned me down and thrown a blanket over my head, so I couldn't see them. They continued to hit me with sticks, and only stopped when my screams alerted my companions in the barrack. By the time help arrived, my assailants had fled. Even though I could not see them, I knew who they were but never had enough proof to confront them directly. I only knew that I had become such a threat that people thought the only way to prevent me from winning was by breaking my legs. This was also the first time I realized there are people who firmly believe in taking short cuts to excel in sports. So while my rivals—in the good old-fashioned way—tried to incapacitate me and take me out of the equation, the sporting cheats of today take much more sophisticated routes. My friends and colleagues had all asked me to identify the attackers, but I remained silent.

Anyway, this incident made me even more determined for the next day's race.

Looking at my wounds, my doctor advised me not to run—he said that the bruises and the swelling needed time to heal, but I was adamant. When I arrived at the starting line, I saw some of the competitors give me startled looks, but only I knew why. But I didn't care. In that moment, all the hardships I had ever faced in the past flashed before my eyes. This was the catharsis I had needed. In that moment I swore to myself I would not let anyone (or anything) come in the way of my *future*. I focused all my energies on running fast. I took off like the wind when I heard the gunshot and easily won the race. I had overcome all odds. I was, however, truly saddened by the viciousness of my attackers, though in some way, my winning had probably given them the worst beating of their lives.

I was selected to represent India at the Olympics in Australia. My joy had no bounds. Here, at last, was the moment I had been waiting, even praying, for. It was my proudest moment yet.

6
From the Bhangra to the Foxtrot

With eager anticipation we awaited the next stage. A tailor was called in to measure us, five boys and one girl, Mary Lila Rao, for the sports kits. We were given blazers, tracksuits, shirts, vests, boots and turbans for the four sardars. I did not know what to expect, or what to hope for—all I knew was that I was filled with happiness, just like a child who had been given a bag full of candy. After all, I would be fulfilling my dream to wear a blazer with INDIA written on it!

A week later, we left for Australia. The night before we left I could not sleep. My small suitcase had been packed with my kit and bedding and I waited for the sun to rise. Excited by the prospects of what lay ahead, we boarded the train to Bombay, the first lap of our long journey across the seas to far-off Australia. We spent three days on the train, singing songs, drinking copious amounts of tea and animatedly discussing the trip. When we reached Bombay's Churchgate station, we were taken by bus to the Astoria hotel. It was the first time that I had seen such a grand place, and I could barely believe my eyes. There was a posh restaurant, a bar and a ballroom where dances were held every night. What was I, a simple village boy doing in such a different world? While we were at the Astoria, Commander Rekhi, our manager, showed us how to knot a tie and gave us lessons on table manners—how to use a napkin and eat with a knife and fork. I have to say that we had great fun manipulating those two implements, trying to pick up pieces of meat and vegetables from our plates and pushing them into our mouths. How much easier it was to eat with our fingers!

On the day of our departure, a deluxe bus waited at the hotel's entrance to take us to Santa Cruz airport. We were told to put our luggage in the bus—only our bedrolls were to be stored at the hotel. I was slightly bemused by that—why do we have to leave our bedding behind? Where would we sleep? What would we do if the nights were chilly? Troubled by these thoughts, I boarded the bus to the airport.

When we reached Santa Cruz, the entire atmosphere at the terminal seemed unreal—its bright lights, the strange sounds, the rush of people. Except for Mary Lila Rao, none of us had flown before. I was scared and confused. I had no bedding and no food. Where would I sleep? What would I eat? How would the plane take off with so many people, their luggage and other cargo? Would it crash under so much weight? I followed my companions towards the huge monster that awaited us, and blindly climbed up the ramp into the cabin. Once inside, like a child, I meekly followed the airhostess to my seat, which was next to Mohinder Singh, our triple and long jumper and another village hick like me. I was asked to fasten my seatbelt, but naturally I did not know what to do and was fumbling with the straps when the airhostess kindly helped me.

When the plane started to taxi along the runway, we both closed our eyes and recited: 'Wahe-Guru, Wahe-Guru.' I had butterflies in my stomach as the plane ascended. And then we were airborne. When I looked out of the window I saw smoke pouring out of the engines, and raised an alarm, thinking that the plane was on fire. The airhostess calmed me down, patiently explaining that it was only the fuel burning. I felt very foolish and laughed with relief.

Our first stop was Singapore. I was awestruck when I saw the airport, by how clean and organized it was, and by the different people all clad in the colourful garments of their respective countries. I had never seen such groups of races and communities before. It was a long flight to Sydney. I tried to sleep, but it was impossible. I was much too excited by what lay ahead. We had a six-hour stopover at Sydney and were given a tour of the city sights. I was shocked when I saw how skimpily dressed the women were and how freely and intimately couples behaved. How different this was from our orthodox society. In the India of the 1950s, it was considered disrespectful for men to look at women directly, or even talk to them. Such free-and-easy ways would definitely be frowned upon. I felt embarrassed watching them and turned my eyes away. At the same time, I realized that customs and norms differed from country to country.

When we arrived at Melbourne, the city that was hosting the Games, we were taken straight to the Olympics Village, where athletes from all over the world were provided with free board and lodging. The rooms were not large but had every amenity that a person would require. What a change from the barracks that had been my home for the past three years!

The Village itself was completely different from the village I grew up in. There was a swimming pool, a state-of-the-art training centre with sophisticated machines, recreational facilities like a cinema, dance hall and reading room, and a restaurant, which dished up a lavish spread for every meal. I had never seen so much food in my life, and yet yearned for the simple desi dal, roti and subzi.

In the evenings, the athletes would dance together in the dance hall. Again it was a culture shock watching men and women holding each other or gyrating to raucous music. I would shyly sit around almost in a trance watching the antics; for me it was both shocking and amusing but what I remember most was how cordial and friendly the atmosphere was. After a while, we also decided to have some fun. Then, regardless of the music that was playing, we would dance the bhangra.

Finally, the historic moment arrived. I proudly took my place in the Indian contingent for the march past. The men were immaculately clad in blue blazers, grey trousers and ties with the Ashok chakra printed on them, while the women wore maroon saris with blue blazers. My dream had come true. Here I was representing India at the Olympics, wearing a blazer with my country's name displayed on the front pocket. The Melbourne Cricket Ground was packed to capacity, spectators clapping and cheering as their favourite athletes and top sporting stars marched past. I felt like a lost child who had strayed into the wrong party, and yet, I wanted to stay on and join in all the fun and games.

Although sports fans in India were getting more familiar with my name and exploits, I was unknown in the international field. The 400-metre race had a hundred and fifty competitors, and for the heats, we were divided into groups of six. The best three in each group were moved up, and the rest eliminated. I was so nervous and overwhelmed that I came last in my group and thus failed to qualify for the next stage. I was deeply disappointed for I had not realized how stiff the competition would be. How could a young and inexperienced athlete like me hope to compete with top international stars? Though this hurdle seemed insurmountable, it made me more determined to prove myself.

At the Village I met several foreign sportspeople, including Charles Jenkins, America's top athlete who had won the gold medal for the 400-metre event at Melbourne. Jenkins was a

great hero of mine and when I heard that he was occupying
the room next door, I was determined to meet him. Although
I had received very basic English lessons from an Anglo-Indian
nurse in Secunderabad, I was not very fluent in it, so enlisted my
roommate Mohinder Singh's help. Jenkins was in the midst of
an interview when we entered his room and invited us to return
the next day. When we finally met him, Mohinder introduced
me in his broken English saying: 'Milkha Singh from India,
400 metres, timing 48 seconds'. He further requested him to
advise me on how to improve my timing. Jenkins kindly wrote
down his complete training schedule for me to follow and from
what he had indicated, a runner could only improve his timing
and technique through regular and rigorous practice. His kind
gesture inspired me and strengthened my desire to excel.

I soon saw how celebrated athletes were and the adulation
that was showered on them almost amounted to hero worship.
Sardars with their turbans attracted a lot of attention and there
were always huge crowds of people outside the Village waiting
to meet us, some insisting that we visit their homes, while others
wanted autographs. I could not understand why small books and
pens were thrust before me, and asked Mohinder what I should
do. He said, just sign your name—that's an autograph—and
so I did, many times over. When we would get back to our
room we would compare notes and ask each other, *'Tu kinne
sign kitte?* (How many did you sign?)' That's how innocent and
naïve we were.

Once the Games ended, we were given a few days off. After
I had been eliminated from the event, an Australian family called

Smith had befriended me. One evening, they invited Mohinder Singh, and me to their home for dinner, but it was only when we reached their house and saw them bringing out the food that we realized what being 'invited for dinner' meant. We had both had our meal at the Village, but didn't know how to communicate this to them. Mohinder tried to tell them in his broken English, or with gestures like rubbing his stomach to indicate we had eaten, but to no avail, and we were forced to have a second meal. After dinner was over, the two daughters, Christine and Mary, asked us to dance. We were embarrassed and said we could not dance. Mr Smith said, 'No problem, our girls will teach you.'

This left us with no option but to accept. We nudged each other, whispering 'you first,' 'no, you first,' awkward at the idea of touching the girls. Boldly, the two sisters came up to us, took our hands and led us to the floor. The gramophone started to play and to the beat of the music, Christine instructed me to 'put your right foot here and say "one", put your left foot there and say "two", one, two, one two…' And so with my left hand resting on her hand and my right arm around her waist, we danced the foxtrot. Gradually my shyness vanished and I began to enjoy myself.

That night when we returned to the Village, Mohinder Singh and I discussed our evening in great detail. We had a good laugh about our 'second dinner', and I teased him, saying, '*Tenu ta angrezi andhi hai* (you claim to know English), so why didn't you say that we had eaten?'

We were both horrified by the parents' laxity, allowing

their daughters to dance so closely with strange men. Such a thing would never ever happen in India. As the days went by, we shed our inhibitions and decided to join in the fun. We invited the girls to the Village and took them to the ballroom. But once there, we did not dare dance with them, so conscious were we by the censure we saw in our fellow Indians' eyes.

We spent five days with the Smith family. They had begun to regard us with affection and even came to see us off at the airport. We promised to keep in touch, but this is not always possible. We were geographically too far apart, and culturally too different.

Our flight back was uneventful. By now, we had grown accustomed to flying and did not panic as we had before. I was returning home with no trophies or medals, just my resolve to be a world champion. From then on, this became my sole purpose in life.

7

My God, My Religion, My Beloved

I returned to India, chastened by my poor performance in Melbourne. I had been so excited by the prospects of being part of the Indian Olympics team, but naïvely, hadn't realized how strong and professional the competition would be. My success in India had filled me with a false sense of pride and it was only when I was on the track that I saw how inconsequential my talents were when pitted against superbly fit and seasoned athletes. It was then that I understood what competition actually meant, and that if I wanted to succeed in the international arena, I must be prepared to test my mettle against the best athletes in the world. I remembered Charles Jenkins' advice that only through regular and rigorous practice can a sportsman improve his technique and build his stamina. In my determination to avoid failure, I set myself a goal to work towards, to transform myself into a running machine.

Between 1956 and 1957, my primary mission in life was to excel in running. The track, to me, was like an open book, in which I could read the meaning and purpose of life. I revered it like I would the sanctum sanctorum in a temple, where the deity resided and before whom I would humbly prostrate myself as a devotee. To keep myself steadfast to my goal, I renounced all pleasures and distractions, to keep myself fit and healthy, and dedicated my life to the ground where I could practise and run.

Running had thus become my God, my religion and my beloved.

My life during those two years was governed by strict rules and regulations and a self-imposed penance. Every morning I would rise at the crack of dawn and after the usual ablutions, would get into my sports kit and dash off to the track, where I would run two or three miles cross-country, in the company of my coach. After the run I would do stretching exercises to develop my muscles.

I followed a similar routine in the evenings—running a couple of miles, jogging between races, and then there would be a cooling-down period. No matter what the weather was, I would practise for five hours every morning and evening, seven days a week, three hundred and sixty-five days a year. It was this disciplined routine that moulded me into the athlete I became. Running had become such an obsession that even when asleep, I would run races in my dreams.

To further build my stamina and strengthen my muscles, I would run long stretches on the sand, or wherever possible, do hill running by going up and down mountain slopes. Three days a week I would lift weights to strengthen my arms, legs and stomach. Sometimes I would play vigorous games like hockey, football or handball, all with the end goal in sight.

I practised so hard and so strenuously that often I was drained of all energy and looked pale as death when the session was complete. There were times when I would increase my speed to such an extent that after my rounds, I would vomit blood or drop down unconscious through sheer exertion. My doctors and coaches warned me, asked me to slow down to maintain my health and equilibrium, but my determination was too strong to give up. My only focus was to become the best athlete in the world.

I recall my practice sessions during the hot summer months of May and June at the National Stadium in Delhi, when temperatures would rise to as high as 45 degrees Celsius. My friends thought I was mad taking such risks, but I refused to let their remarks or the weather daunt me. I would run round after round under the blistering sun and when I would pause for a rest, I could feel the heat radiating from my body and my vest would be dripping with sweat. I would then pull it off and wring it dry into a bucket. By the time I had finished practice, the bucket would be filled with my sweat, and I would be lying prostrate on the ground, totally exhausted. In desperation I would cry out, 'Wahe-Guru, ais wari mainoo bachha lo aur main aae phir kadi nahi karanga! (Oh God, save me this time and I will never do this to myself again!)' But then images of packed stadiums filled with cheering spectators, wildly applauding me as I crossed the finishing line, would flash across my mind and I would start again, encouraged by visions of victory.

I had learnt the hard way that the road to success was not easy, and that I would encounter many obstacles and barriers along the way. Yet, I had intentionally embarked upon this difficult journey, driven by my desire to succeed. At heart, I was still that impoverished boy who ran to school in his bare feet and who had courageously challenged fate.

My perseverance and tenacity were relentless. Besides, I firmly believed that if a person worked hard and with sincerity, his efforts would be rewarded. My coach during these years was Ranbir Singh, who would observe my every move and action to see that I adhered to the programme he had prepared.

In my experience, the relationship between a coach and a trainee has to be based on extreme trust. He is your guide, your mentor and also your sternest critic. A coach should be a hard taskmaster and discipline you if the need arises; after all, it is he who controls your career as an athlete. All the coaches who have trained me, including Gurdev Singh, Baldev Singh, Ranbir Singh and Dr Howard, have been sources of great inspiration and motivation for me. In fact, it was because of Dr Howard's motivation that I won the gold at Cardiff. I will always be grateful to them.

My strenuous training programme had to be supplemented by a balanced, high-protein diet to make up for the nutrients lost during practice. I avoided fatty substances like butter and ghee, and instead, drank glasses of milk and ate plenty of green vegetables, fruit, eggs, fish and lean meat. I would never eat the same meals every day, but would vary the ingredients and combinations to help digestion. There is nothing more ruinous than a sportsman with diarrhoea.

One of the maxims I have always followed was early to bed and early to rise, because rest and sleep help raise energy levels. I lived an austere, almost monkish life, abiding by the rules I had set for myself. I shunned late nights and never indulged in bad habits like smoking, drinking or too much caffeine—I have seen the impact such addictions have had on athletes, how they affect speed and reduce muscle power.

As my fame grew, so did the attention I received from my fans, both men and women. Huge crowds would follow me wherever I went, and often I would find that the girls outnumbered boys. At times their boldness would embarrass me, but there were also moments when I would feel flattered by their admiration. But one of my rules was to avoid any close relationships with the opposite sex. Starting a romance in those days was not an option for me; I did not want any complications in my life then. I was convinced that I didn't want any distractions that would keep me away from my goal. Besides, I was still young, and in no hurry to find a soul mate.

I had the full support of the army during these years when my demanding practice routine had taken over my life. My regiment gave me extra food and milk and I was exempted from regular military duties so that I could concentrate on my training. My victories made my regiment very happy, more so because by setting new records, I was also bringing glory to the armed forces.

8
Going for Gold

In 1957, my career was an unbroken record of victories. I participated in all sports tournaments, ranging from regimental events to All-India meets, establishing new All-India records. At the Bangalore National Games, I won both the 400- and 200-metre races, clocking 47.5 seconds for the former and 21.3 seconds for the latter. As a result, my name became well known throughout the country, not only in sports circles but in every household.

The next year, 1958, was a glorious one for me, one that I firmly believe was the year of my destiny. My coach was an American called Dr Howard, who taught me an advanced technique of taking a start. Once again, there was the usual cycle of events. My demanding routine had brought the expected results and I was now a running machine, breaking the records I had set the previous year—clocking 46.2 seconds for 400 metres and 21.2 seconds for 200 metres—at the National Games held at the Barabatti Stadium in Cuttack. Other runners lagged far behind me. Seemingly, I had broken the previous Asian record in 400 metres, but I found my new record hard to believe and requested the National Games' organizing committee to measure the track again. They did so and I was assured that my timings were correct.

My new record had created a stir not only in India but also throughout Asia. I intensified my practice, bearing in mind that the 1958 Asian Games in Tokyo were due to take place a few months later. Although the Indian contingent was large, all eyes were fixed on me.

In May, our team left Calcutta for Tokyo. I was thrilled to have been given a chance to visit Japan, a country I admired for the tenacious way they had rehabilitated themselves after the devastation wrought by the Second World War. When we landed at Tokyo airport, our eyes were dazzled by the brightness of the multicoloured lights. The puddles of water that had collected after a recent shower glowed with the reflection of the lights as well. As we deplaned, we saw hordes of reporters, press photographers and cameramen waiting outside. They had heard that Milkha Singh had arrived, and wanted to know who he was. In response, India's chef-de-mission, Ashwini Kumar, presented me to the press, saying, 'This is Milkha Singh.' Cameras flashed and microphones were thrust before me as I was surrounded by dozens of reporters. I was made to stand in front of the other athletes as a newsreel was shot. Fortunately, I did not have to answer any of the questions that I was bombarded with—they were all taken care of by Mr Kumar and Baldev Singh, our coach.

I boarded the deluxe bus, still bemused by the reception I had received. Our bus was escorted by two smart young men, dressed in black outfits and white caps, riding motorcycles, with lights flashing and sirens blaring as we raced through the city. When we reached Diatchi hotel, the place we were staying, hordes of people had gathered outside, waiting for me. I was mobbed when I got off the bus, some people even thrust autograph books at me. Suddenly, Mr Kumar was at my side. He grabbed my arm and led me away, saying, 'Please don't get distracted by all this. Concentrate on your practice and the event. I have collected the autograph books and you can sign them in your room. I will return them to their owners.' He then turned to the crowds and said, 'I request you all to please excuse us so that the athletes can settle down in their rooms and rest after their long journey.'

When we entered the hotel, the receptionist greeted us, saying, 'We have received many telephonic enquiries about Milkha Singh. Kindly give us a time when we can hold a press conference.'

Mr Kumar replied, 'We have just arrived after a long journey and are tired, so at this moment it will not be possible for Milkha Singh to meet anyone. We request all well-wishers to excuse us for now. If they can come to the hotel tomorrow morning at 11, Milkha Singh will be at their disposal.'

My roommate on this trip was Parduman Singh, who had for many years been the Indian and Asian champion for shot-put and discus. We were both gratified by the affection that we had received but could not understand why this was so.

In the bathroom, I looked at my face in the mirror—my eyes were bloodshot and I looked tired. At the same time I was flushed with joy. I smiled at my reflection, wondering how an ordinary person like me could receive such a hero's welcome. I soaked in the tub for a while and then went to the dining room. When I entered, I saw flashes of recognition on the faces of the other diners and was greeted warmly by everyone. My English was still weak, even after all the lessons I had received, and I found it difficult to respond to their queries.

At the dining table, Mr Kumar told us all about Tokyo and its famous sights, its clubs, nightlife and fast-paced lifestyle. He warned us not to leave the hotel at night, and said that whoever disobeyed this order, would face strict disciplinary action and be sent back home. He added that after the Games, we would be allowed to stay on and then we could do what we liked. His warning was timely, because Japanese society, like Australia's, was open and sexually progressive. We retired to our rooms early because we had to report for practice at 8 a.m. the next morning.

At 7 a.m. our doorbell rang. When I opened the door I saw a pretty girl, all dressed in white, standing there holding a tea tray in her hands. She bowed and politely wished me 'Good morning.' She entered the room, put the tray down and asked me, 'How much sugar do you take? Would you prefer milk or a slice of lemon?' When I repeated what she had asked to Parduman, he protested, saying, 'She has not wished me "good morning". Tell her to send another girl up to serve me tea.'

The poor girl looked bewildered, so I asked her to sit down and explained. Smilingly, she poured the tea and handed the cups to us. As we chatted, I discovered that she, like many other young girls, came from good families and worked at the hotel to earn money so they could continue their education. They cleaned the rooms, made beds, washed and ironed clothes, as well as did other chores that made a hotel guest's stay comfortable.

After we drank our tea, we changed into our running kits and left by bus for the stadium that was about three miles away. Teams from all over Asia had collected on the grounds, practising with great enthusiasm—I was electrified by the highly charged atmosphere. When we walked in, all eyes were turned towards us. Cameras clicked as I started to warm-up. Film units took action photographs of me from different angles. We practised for two hours and then returned to the hotel for the press conference.

For about forty-five minutes, the journalists asked me numerous questions: 'When did you start taking part in races?' 'When did you get interested in sports?' 'What are your hobbies?' And so on and so forth. My answers were basic, and I'm sure, not quite what they expected. One of them even invited me for dinner, another for drinks.

It was at our hotel that I first met Abdul Khaliq, a member

of the Pakistani team. Baldev Singh introduced us, saying, 'Meet Abdul Khaliq, the world-renowned sprinter in 100 and 200 metres. And this is Milkha Singh, our racing star. Beware of him, he's a fiend in 200 metres.' In annoyance, Khaliq shot back, 'I have met and run races with many a Tom, Dick and Harry like him. They are no match for me.' I was completely unprepared for such a spiteful attack, and thought to myself, 'Why is he being so rude? India may have been partitioned, but we still belong to the same race. Surely, he could not have forgotten our traditional norms of courtesy and tameez?'

In the days before the Games were due to open, the newspapers carried glowing accounts of my achievements and career, accompanied by large photographs on the front page. I was deeply gratified by the publicity I had received and hoped that I would be able to live up to their expectations.

At last the opening day arrived. All the participating nations had gathered at the stadium, waiting for the opening ceremony to begin. When the band started to play, it was a signal for the march past to commence. The Indian contingent, smartly clad in blue blazers, grey trousers, white shirts and blue ties with the Ashok chakra printed on them, were led by a beautiful Japanese girl wearing a blue sari and carrying our national flag. As each team passed in front of the saluting base, they dipped their colours before Emperor Hirohito of Japan, who then declared the Games open. The jubilant spectators cheered, waving multicoloured flags, thousands of balloons were released and fireworks burst to mark the memorable occasion. And then there was a hush as a veteran Japanese athlete, Mikio

Oda, ran into the stadium carrying aloft a burning torch—an Olympics tradition that was introduced at the Tokyo Asiad. He encircled the stadium and then placed the torch on a specially made stand in front of the emperor. The torch, a symbol of steadfastness, sportsmanship and good luck, was kept lit throughout the duration of the Games, protected by armed guards. The torchbearer then made a reverse turn and left the stadium, followed by the marching teams.

The 400-metre race was held the next day. Several of my fellow competitors, whose timing was more than mine, came up to me to ask for advice and I was happy to offer them some quick tips. I had practised hard and ran the race in a very relaxed manner. I not only won the race, but also set a new Asian Games record.

My heart was bursting with pride as I stood at the first position on the victory stand. On my right and left were the second and third place winners from Japan and the Philippines respectively. The emperor walked slowly towards the stand, flanked by military guards, and led by three beautiful girls carrying trays in which the gold, silver and bronze medals were ensconced. When the emperor stood in front of me, the loudspeakers announced that Milkha Singh from India had won the 400-metre race, clocking 46.5 seconds, a new record for Asia. The audience erupted with joy, cheering and applauding. I felt my hair stand on end and a shiver of delight ran through me. With a smile, the emperor held out his hand, which I happily shook. I then bent my head and he draped the gold medal around my neck. He followed the same procedure for the other two. When the ceremony was over, we all turned towards the flagpoles to watch the flags of India, Japan and the Philippines go up as the band played the national anthems of the three nations. The entire audience of a hundred thousand people rose as one to honour our flags and anthems. It was the most stirring moment in my life and I was filled with great patriotic fervour just seeing the Tricolour fluttering in the open blue sky. Overcome with emotion, I closed my eyes for a moment, thinking that it was for this flag and for our motherland that thousands of martyrs (shaheeds) and patriots had suffered and sacrificed themselves. Then the realization hit me that this was not only my triumph—my success had brought glory to my country as well.

When I returned to the hotel, I found hundreds of congratulatory messages waiting for me. My victory had affected each member of the Indian contingent and our mood was upbeat that evening. Friends and colleagues would come up to me, pat me on my back, and praise my performance. The next morning, I was headline news:

MILKHA THRILLS CROWDS
THE REFUGEE WHO ROSE TO STARDOM
MAGNIFICENT EFFORT BY MILKHA: SETS NEW 400-METRE MARK

I was thrilled to see my photographs in the newspapers and to read about my exploits, but only for a short while—I still had another crucial event ahead of me.

The 200-metre race would take place the next day in which I would be competing against the Pakistani champion, Abdul

Khaliq. Many thought I could not win, but my spirits were high, buoyed by my victory and the encouragement I had received from my well-wishers. All through the night before the race, I was consumed by an intense desire to defeat Khaliq so that I could be declared Asia's best athlete. The criterion for winning the title was clear: both Abdul Khaliq and I were at the same position, he had won the 100-metre race and I the 400-metre one, and this event would be decisive in proving who was the better athlete.

When we reached the stadium, we both did warm-up exercises in preparation for the race, which was to be held in the afternoon. I was in a fever of anxiety when the call for the race came, a feeling all athletes experience before a major event. The six of us finalists stood at the starting line in our shorts and vests. Khaliq got the outer lane and I the inner one. We wished each other good luck, a mere formality neither of us meant. The gun was fired and the race began. The spectators held their breath, watching, waiting... We both completed the first 100 metres and were running in tandem, our steps parallel. Despite focusing on our running, we were each aware of the other's progress and were pushing ourselves and our utmost limits. It was fast, it was furious, it was neck-to-neck. Then there was high drama. About three or four yards from the finishing line, I pulled a muscle on my right leg. Then my legs got entangled and I tripped and tumbled over the finishing line. At that very moment, Khaliq breasted the tape too. Fortunately for me, the cameras had photographed every movement at the finishing line from different angles, but we still had to wait half-an-hour for the verdict as the organizers needed time to develop the pictures for adjudicating the photo finish. For thirty minutes, the longest in my life, we did not know who had won. Then came the long-awaited result—I had won! Khaliq was devastated. I, on the other hand, was on top of the world—by winning my second gold medal I was now Asia's best athlete!

Once again I stood at the first place on the victory stand, with Khaliq on the second and a Japanese athlete at the third place. Professor G.D. Sondhi, a member of the Indian Olympic Committee, placed the gold medal around my neck. I felt like reminding Khaliq about 'Tom, Dick and Harry', but that was not my style.

With this victory I had entered the select group of Asia's top athletes. My fame had spread quickly, with headlines proclaiming: *MILKHA RUNS 200 METRES IN RECORD TIME.* I returned to my room and once again found scores of congratulatory messages, letters and telegrams waiting for me. As I looked at them, I thought about how far I had travelled from my obscure little village in Pakistan, and a sense of loss suddenly came upon me as vivid images from my life flashed through my mind—my father's and brothers' deaths, my mother's anguished cries from inside the burning gurudwara, the horrors of Partition, bloodshed and slaughter, the train to Delhi, despair, suffering, poverty, rejection, struggles, the days of crime on the streets, ten days in jail, a lucky break in the army, life in the barracks, my chance encounter with running, my relentless training schedule, my sacrifices, my goal, lady luck smiling on me, fame and recognition, hero-worship by the loving masses… My dreams had become reality… The rush of emotions overwhelmed me and I put my head down and sobbed like a child. The storms had steeled me, but the glories of the present had rocked me back into dark visions of the past. But the stream of life moves on.

Parduman Singh, who had won the gold in shot-put and silver in discus, returned to the room in good humour. Listening to him speak and laughing at his jokes was like a tonic and I began to feel more cheerful again. As we talked, the phone kept ringing and there were frequent knocks at the door as my fellow athletes, including some Pakistani athletes from Punjab, came in to congratulate me. This spirit of camaraderie, particularly from the Pakistanis, dispelled some of the rancour of our bloodstained past.

That night, we attended the Emperor's banquet at the Imperial Palace and I was formally introduced to His Highness, who graciously said, through an interpreter, 'We were pleased to watch your run. If you continue your efforts you will become the world's number one champion.' I humbly thanked him for his kind words of encouragement and diffidently replied, saying that my success was due to the love and encouragement extended to me by the people of Japan.

For the closing ceremony on the next day, we assembled once again at the stadium as the Japanese bid us sayonara. Electronic boards displayed messages in both Japanese and English that said: 'We have done our utmost to make these Games a success. Please forgive us for any inadequacies, and do visit our city and country again.' Towards the end of the show, the lights dimmed and children in rainbow-coloured clothes holding flaming torches performed a wonderful dance. It was a magical conclusion to a memorable event.

Fans were waiting for us at the hotel and the moment we descended from the bus, we were mobbed by scores of eager and well-meaning boys and girls. Some brought us little tokens and gifts while others just wanted autographs. I was touched by their love and affection.

Parduman Singh and I wanted to buy presents for the young girls at the hotel, but they surprised us by giving us dolls and other small objects. We thanked them in Japanese: *'arigatou gozaimasu'*, we offer our thanks to you. They were delighted. In return we gave them scarves and some brass curios we had brought from India. We had grown very fond of them and when we left, they came to the airport to see us off.

9
Meeting Pandit Nehru

We returned to India via Hong Kong, where we spent four nights. Hong Kong was a vibrant city with a swinging nightlife. However, my vow of self-control remained steadfast and I was not tempted by what I saw.

We landed in Calcutta to a tumultuous welcome. And then it was on to Delhi. As we entered the airport building, a band started to play and well-wishers rushed up to garland us and offer us sweets, felicitating us for the many gold, silver and bronze medals we had brought back with us. Invitations from the president, Dr Rajendra Prasad, prime minister, Pandit Jawaharlal Nehru, defence minister and the chief of army staff poured in.

Panditji held a grand reception in honour of the Indian team on the lawns of his imposing residence, Teen Murti Bhavan, which was attended by cabinet ministers, government officials and high-ranking officers from the armed forces. He received us graciously, warmly shaking our hands. When I was presented to him, he gave me a friendly smile and then embraced me. I was elated that such a great man had greeted me so fondly.

Panditji asked me to sit next to him at one of the tables. 'My boy,' he said to me, 'you have brought great pride to our country. If you keep up the hard work, you will be one of the world's top athletes.'

'Panditji, my interest in running was awakened recently, and I have taken an oath to persevere until I attain the goal I have set for myself.'

The prime minister was pleased by my reply, and asked me to tell him about myself. When I narrated the story of my past and the tragedy of losing most of my family during Partition, he reassured me in a voice choked with emotion, 'I cannot change the past nor bring the dead back to life, but remember my boy, you are not an orphan. I, and many Indians my age, are your father and mother. If you are even in need of anything, you must come to me.'

He then told General Thimayya, the chief of army staff, to take special care of me.

At Defence Minister V.K. Krishna Menon's reception the next day, it was announced that all gold medallists would be promoted immediately, an unprecedented move that elevated me from a sepoy to the rank of a junior commissioned officer

(JCO). This promotion was a huge jump in my career. If I hadn't won two gold medals, I would probably have remained a sepoy or risen to the rank of a havaldar at the most. Now thanks to the decision taken by the defence minister and chief of army staff, a new military tradition had been initiated, where it was mandatory that all soldiers who received gold medals in international events would be promoted automatically. What a tremendous incentive this would be for future sportsmen!

On the third evening, at General Thimayya's reception, my promotion became a reality. All of us who had received gold medals stood in a straight line while we waited for our names to be called. When it was my turn, the general called for the stars and ceremoniously fixed one on each of my epaulets. He congratulated me saying, 'The honour of the army and the nation is now in your hands. I have ordered your unit to provide you with special facilities.'

After the function, I returned to my lodgings at my unit. My promotion had filled me with such pride that I refused to remove my uniform and, wherever I went, I was saluted by jawans—a novel experience for me. Throughout my army life I had been saluting my seniors, and now, here I was, being saluted at. Such are the ironies of life!

I returned to my unit in Secunderabad after a few days. As the plane was hovering over the airport, a flood of emotions swept over me. This was the place where I had begun my career, where I had made a solemn pledge that one day I, too, would represent my country in international tournaments, where coaches like Gurdev Singh had given me the confidence to compete, succeed and move ahead. I remembered my late-night practices and the sacrifices I had made. The insignificant jawan was now returning as a hero! But I would never let success go to my head. My past helped keep me grounded and I remained focussed on higher goals.

Thousands of jawans, officers and the general public were impatiently waiting for me at the airport. When the plane taxied to a halt, I emerged from the cabin and waved to the waiting crowds, who cheered me vociferously. The military band started to play as I slowly descended. Brigadier G.S. Bal, our commanding officer, came up to greet me, while cameras flashed. Jawans presented the guard of honour and I proudly took the salute. With my face covered by garlands of marigolds, roses and jasmine, I walked alongside Brigadier Bal and other officers, down the red carpet lined by cheering jawans dressed in their best uniforms.

Tea was served at the airport, and throughout the time we were there, officers and their families kept coming up to me, eager to know more about my victories in Tokyo. The band preceded me as I came out of the building, where an open jeep awaited me. I sat between Brigadier Bal and Colonel Bhave, as our cavalcade slowly moved through the twin cities of Hyderabad and Secunderabad until we reached the unit. The roads were lined with local citizens, as well as jawans who smartly saluted us. It was flowers, flowers all the way. My joy was limitless and I was filled with gratitude for the affection and respect I had received. God had been more than good to me.

༄

10
'Come on, Singh'

I spent a few days at the EME Centre before the next major sporting event—the Sixth British Empire and Commonwealth Games a few months later. It was initially known as the British Empire Games and was renamed to the British Empire and Commonwealth Games in 1954 and the British Commonwealth Games in 1970, before finally gaining its current title, the Commonwealth Games, in 1978.

I had resumed my practice schedule soon after I returned from Tokyo and when it was confirmed that I was part of the Indian team, I was filled with both joy and trepidation. Joy at the thought of competing with some of the best athletes in the world, trepidation because I was uncertain about the outcome. Friends and well-wishers who came to see me off at Delhi airport were all very supportive and repeatedly remarked that they had great hopes of me returning with another gold medal. But in my present state of apprehension and self-doubt, this seemed a formidable task.

We landed in London and after a brief stopover left by train for Cardiff in Wales, where the Games were to be held. On the train we were informed that for part of our journey we would be travelling through a tunnel that had been built under the River Severn. I was flabbergasted by this fact and wondered what amazing engineering feat had created this underwater tunnel.

At Cardiff, we were received by representatives of the organizing committee and taken to the military base where we, along with the other teams, were staying. In the evening we were taken to the Cardiff Arms Park for practice. There I saw athletes who looked stronger and sturdier than I. Some even seemed seven feet tall! Compared to them I was like a pigmy among giants. All the press reporters and cameramen were clustered around athletes of international repute and no one paid me the slightest notice. My fame was restricted to Asia, but here I was just another participant in the midst of eminent sportsmen from about thirty-five nations who formed the Commonwealth.

Three days later, Her Majesty Queen Elizabeth declared the Games open, and the specially designed Commonwealth flag was ceremonially raised. The Queen's Baton, which she had handed over at Buckingham Palace and which had then been carried by a relay of runners to Cardiff, was presented to Prince Philip, the Duke of Edinburgh, so that he could read the Queen's message to the assembled participants and audience. The Queen's Baton, which is so much a part of the Commonwealth Games today, was launched at Cardiff.

Our American coach, Dr Howard, had accompanied the Indian team. He was an outstanding trainer, who was very well acquainted with international training patterns and techniques. He was also very astute and could easily judge the strengths and weaknesses of the other athletes. For an entire day he mentored me, giving me pointers on what to expect. More than anything, he was trying to rid me of my inferiority complex and instil self-belief. I had convinced myself that there was no way that I could be amongst the six finalists, let alone win a gold medal. What chance did I have against superbly fit professionals like Malcolm Spence from South Africa, George Kerr from Jamaica, Kevan Gosper from Australia, Terry Tobacco from Canada and John Salisbury from England.

However, because of Dr Howard's motivation and advice, I won heat after heat, and effortlessly reached the finals. The night before the race, Dr Howard reiterated the tips he had drilled into me. He revealed that Spence had more stamina than speed, and that I should stick to my own style of running the 400-metre race, that is, to start in top gear. He emphasized that I must not start slowly, that I must maintain my speed for the first 300 metres, and then give it my all in the last 100 metres. He said that if I ran the first 300 metres at full speed, Spence would do the same, although that was not his running strategy.

The morale-boosting attitude and clever strategies Howard gave me, equipped me with the confidence I badly needed. I started believing that I could be the best. Another constant motivation was a burning desire to do well for the country—I was well aware that my good performance would lead to the glory of India.

In spite of all my positive thoughts, I spent another sleepless night before the race, tormented by nightmares of what could go wrong. My confidence again had plummeted and I wondered what I should do—participate or quit. The lack of sleep and my morbid thoughts had drained me. The race was scheduled for 4 p.m. in the afternoon. I got up at the usual time, soaked in a tub of hot water to relax, had breakfast and then fell back into bed and covered myself with a blanket. After a refreshing nap, I awoke at noon, had a meagre meal of a cup of soup and a couple of slices of bread. I did not want to overeat, in case it would impact upon my performance.

At 1 p.m., I combed and knotted my long hair on the top of my head and covered it with a white kerchief. In my Air India bag, I packed my spiked shoes, a small towel, a comb and a packet of glucose. Then I put on my tracksuit, and closed my eyes in meditation, conjuring up images of Guru Nanak, Guru Gobind Singh and Lord Shiva. I silently and fervently prayed to them to give me strength and to guide me through what lay ahead.

My other team members were waiting for me on the bus. When I took my seat, they jokingly remarked: 'Today, Milkha Singh is off colour.' 'Well my friend, what is the matter?' 'Why are you not happy?' I did not respond to their wisecracks and humour, but it did lighten my mood. All my thoughts and emotions were focused on the forthcoming event.

Sensing my nervousness, Howard came and sat next to me. Encouragingly he said, 'Milkha Singh, today's race will make or mar you, it will either put you up or pull you down. Such a chance will not come your way for another four years and four years is a long time. It is now or never. If you follow my tips, you will beat Malcolm Spence. This feat is not beyond your capacity.' His words raised my spirits, somewhat.

When we reached the stadium I went to the dressing room and lay down, agitated and disturbed. I felt feverish and queasy, sick both in mind and body. At 3 p.m., Howard came to me, rubbed my back and massaged my legs. He said, 'My boy, get ready. Your race begins in an hour.'

I reached the track, put down my bag and, like the other competitors, began my warm-up exercises. Throughout the waiting period, Howard stood beside me, murmuring words of encouragement.

The first call for the 400-metre race came at 3.50 p.m. The six of us reported at the starting line and were made to stand in a row. As we stood there, I heard voices calling, 'Come on, Singh; come on, Singh'. I wiped the sweat from my legs with my towel and was tying the laces of my spiked boots when the second call came. I removed my tracksuit and stood there in my shorts and vest emblazoned with the word INDIA under the Ashok chakra. I took a few deep breaths. The six of us went through the usual courtesy of wishing each other good luck.

Salisbury was in the first lane, Spence in the second, Kerr in the third, Gosper in the fourth, Tobacco in the fifth, and finally I in the last one. My heart was pounding wildly. When the starter said 'On your mark', I got into the starting position, with my left foot just behind the starting line, my right knee parallel to my left foot and both hands touching the ground.

I invoked the blessings of the Almighty once again while I waited for the signal. The gun went off with a loud bang and as we took off there were loud cheers and claps from the spectators, some backing Spence, some Gosper, while the majority were yelling for Salisbury.

I ran as if the furies were after me. I remembered Howard's advice and strained every muscle for the first 300 metres. I was in the lead and when Spence saw that I was running at lightning speed, he tried to overtake me, but luck was on my side. I saw the white tape when I was just fifty yards away and made a mighty push to reach it before Spence caught up. There was a gap of a yard or so between us when I floated ahead and breasted the tape. Wild cries of 'Come on, Singh; come on, Singh', filled the air. I had won the race!

And then, my body felt lifeless and I fell to the ground unconscious. The effort I had put into the race had taken its toll. From what I later heard, I was taken on a stretcher to the medical post, where I was revived with oxygen.

It was only after I regained consciousness that the realization that I had won started sinking in. My teammates and other supporters surrounded me and lifted me on to their shoulders. As they brought me back to the stadium from the medical post, thunderous cheers greeted me. I draped the Indian flag around me and took a victory lap of the stadium.

After my race, I was interviewed by BBC television.

'Mr Singh, how do feel after winning the race?
'I felt nothing at all, I was lost in another world. Now I feel just like any other winner in my position—on top of the world!'

'Did you hope to win the race?'
'I had no such hope. I only tried to do my best and I am happy that I succeeded beyond my expectations.'

'In your hour of victory, do you have any messages for your country?'
'Only to say: my country, your son has done his duty towards you. May every citizen do his duty to his motherland.'

'What are your impressions about the people of this country?'
'Their love and good wishes inspired me to win.' (This reply was just a formality.)

'Did you have a chance to run with these athletes before?'
'No, this is the first time that I have had the honour.'

My win was a historic event, particularly significant because this was the first time that an Indian athlete had won a gold medal at the Commonwealth Games. My victory had put India on the sports map of the world.

When I first arrived in Cardiff I was a nonentity. Today, I was treated like a celebrity. Our high commissioner to the Court of St James, Mrs Vijaylakshmi Pandit, had watched my win from the VIP enclosure, and she came up to congratulate me after the victory ceremony. When I saw her approach, escorted by our manager Ashwini Kumar, I wondered who that lady with 'bob-cut' hair was. Then we were introduced and I was very happy to meet the sister of our prime minister, Pandit Nehru, whom I had had the privilege of meeting after I had returned from Tokyo. She embraced me and remarked that I had raised India's honour and the nation was proud of me. I was uplifted by such warm felicitations. Then she told me that Panditji had sent a message asking what I would like as a reward for bringing such glory to India. I requested that a national holiday be declared on the day I landed in India—a wish that the prime minister happily granted! The Duke of Edinburgh had also come up to greet me. He had watched me winning the race and said, 'I greatly appreciate Milkha Singh's style of running.'

That night we met sportsmen from all the other Commonwealth nations. We congratulated each other and talked of this and that. The next morning, I received a tsunami of telegrams praising my performance and congratulating me for winning.

After the Games ended, we left for London where we stayed at the Dorchester Hotel. Queen Elizabeth had invited all the teams who had participated in the Games for a grand banquet at Buckingham Palace. We were all awestruck by the invitation, well aware of how prestigious it was for us humble athletes to be given the opportunity to visit the Queen's palatial residence and mingle with a distinguished guest line-up of royalty, ministers, diplomats and celebrities. When our team arrived at the palace, smartly clad in our blue blazers—and us sardars in turbans—we attracted the attention of the glamorous crowd. A ball was held after the banquet. By then the guests had congregated in groups and drinks were served. I had my first ever sip of beer that evening and was bold enough to join the dancing couples on the floor. After all, I had received good practice in this area in Australia. The Indian contingent was amused, but I egged them on to join in. I said, 'Today is a day of great rejoicing and no one should disapprove of dancing at such an occasion.' My words acted as an incentive and my companions joined in the festivities. While we were dancing, the lights dimmed and some couples got closer and more intimate with their partners. When the lights came on, we were all amused to see that many of the young men had traces of lipstick on their lips. Such behaviour is unacceptable in India, but this was the West.

We left for Delhi the next morning, where once again I was received rapturously. What was even more gratifying was that my arrival was celebrated with a national holiday!

I was a star, my name a household word and the stories of my exploits had acquired legendary proportions. My struggles and perseverance had finally heaped huge rewards, not only for me but for my country as well.

11
The Flying Sikh

My triumph at the Commonwealth Games had elevated my status to such a level that I was now an international sports celebrity. Between 1958 and 1960 I received numerous invitations from different countries and travelled throughout the world, participating in at least eighty international races, out of which I won seventy-seven. The international press featured glowing articles on my life and achievements, because wherever I went I broke the old 400-metre records, establishing new ones.

In 1960, the much-awaited Olympic Games was to take place in Rome. I was very excited; this would be my second

Olympics after Melbourne in 1956. In the years since then, I had matured and grown as an athlete, and was now at my peak. Perhaps I would have better luck this time.

But, before that, in January, I was to participate in the National Games at Delhi's National Stadium. My sister Isher and her family were very keen to see me run. They had heard of my exploits but had never watched me on the track. I happily invited them for the event. I was overjoyed to see them, especially my beloved sister Isher, who had sold her gold earrings to secure my release from jail all those years ago. When I greeted her, she said, 'Dear brother, you have endured terrible hardships and trials, but now good fortune has smiled upon you, and us because of you. Don't get exhausted by running so fast.' Her love and concern overwhelmed me and I embraced her warmly, at the same time assuring her that running did not debilitate my body; instead it gave me added strength.

She responded with tears in her eyes, 'My dear brother, your name is like a shining star in the world today. You have raised the honour of our family enormously. If only our parents were alive to see what you have achieved. How happy and proud they would have been.' I wiped her tears gently and tried to console her, 'Who can fight fate? Perhaps I would never have reached such pinnacles of success if I hadn't endured those early days of austerity and adversity.'

My sister was unaware of the little surprise I had planned for her. I asked her to put on my India blazer. Once she did, I asked her to put her hands in the side pockets of the blazer. I had put a gold earring in each of the pockets. 'These are for you',

I told her. She took the earrings and just couldn't stop crying.

Inside the stadium, I ordered tea and fruit for my family, but Isher demurred saying, 'Why are you going through all this trouble for us? We've already had tea.' Her simple remarks filled me with affection as I led them into the stadium. As we entered, I felt the crowd staring at their simple attire with disdain. For a moment I felt embarrassed, but then was filled with loathing at people's snobbish attitudes. With great love and consideration I made them sit in the best seats and stayed with them until my event began.

Isher asked me where I would run and I pointed to the track, and patiently explained that the athlete who would reach the winning post first would receive a medal, which added to his glory as a sportsman. When I entered the field, Isher tried to keep her eyes fixed on me throughout the duration of the race. I came first as usual, but fainted yet again because of the energy I had expended while running. My poor sister thought that I had been shot dead by the gun that had started the race. She started wailing loudly when she saw me being carried away on a stretcher. The other spectators attempted to reassure her, but she was not convinced and demanded that she be taken to me immediately. When she saw me lying down looking pale, with a film of glucose on my lips, she cried, 'I can't bear to see you in this condition. *Veer* (brother), please, I beg you, give up running.'

When I recovered, we returned to the stadium to be greeted by vociferous cheers. I nudged Isher and remarked, 'Look at the honour and praise I receive when I run and win races. If I stop running, no one will bother about me.' But she was still not convinced.

The National Games were held for three days, during which I set new records—100 metres (10.4); 200 metres (20.8); 400 metres (46.1); 4x100-metre relay (42.1); and 4x400-metre relay (3.12.6).

Soon after the National Games, our team had received an invitation from the Pakistani government for the Indo-Pak Sports Meet. What an ironic twist of fate. I was returning to the land where I was born, where I had lost my home and most of my family in the inhuman savagery that followed Partition. It was not the religious bigotry that troubled me, just the fear that the visit would revive those horrible memories. I did not want to go, but Pandit Nehru intervened, saying that this visit was for the honour of our country and that I was going there as an ambassador for India. The others in our team felt as I did, as we reluctantly travelled to the border at Attari via Amritsar. The welcoming committee at the border greeted us warmly and then we were taken by bus to the Faletti's Hotel in Lahore.

Days before the Meet opened, headlines in newspapers as well as banners and posters carried large-print notices that said:

'Indo-Pak Athlete Duel
Abdul Khaliq to meet Milkha Singh'

The Meet was declared open by the president of Pakistan, General Ayub Khan, at the newly constructed Gaddafi Stadium. There were more than thirty thousand spectators in the men's enclosure, and several thousand more of burqa-clad ladies in the

With Sardar Kairon in Chandigarh

A family portrait

With close friend, Virdi

The loving couple

Relaxing

Supporting young sporting talent in Punjab

With Rani Mukherjee and Abhishek Bachchan

With (front row, from left to right) Shiny Abraham-Wilson, Kanwaljit Sandhu, Tina Ambani, P.T. Usha and my wife

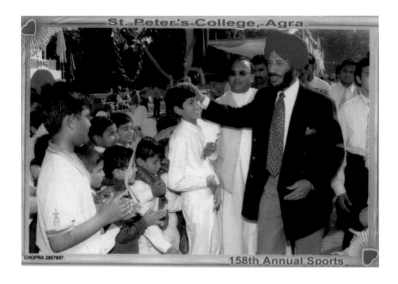

Supporting young sporting talent

With Dr Karan Singh

With (from left to right) Prasoon Joshi, Lady Aruna Paul, Baron Swraj Paul,
Farhan Akhtar, Sonam Kapoor and Rakeysh Omprakash Mehra

women's. The general, other senior officials and their families sat comfortably in the Presidential Box.

At this event I was once again pitted against my old opponent, Abdul Khaliq, whom I had defeated at the Tokyo games.

Consequently, the massive crowd's excitement levels were high as they eagerly waited for the moment when their hero would defeat me. In this Meet, too, the pattern of our victories were the same as at Tokyo—Khaliq won the 100 metres and I, the 400-metre race. The deciding race would be the 200-metre one. My teammates reassured me by saying that there was no way that I could lose, my technique was too finely honed and my timing was much better than the one at Tokyo. But as usual, on the day of the race, I woke up feeling feverish and bilious. I was shivering, either because I was unwell or by memories of those terrible days that still haunted me. Instead of succumbing or feeling sorry for myself, I forced myself to get up and go to the stadium. As I said to myself, over and over again, I had to win because a defeat in Pakistan would be a fate worse than death.

The Pakistanis had heard about me, but only because I had defeated their hero two years ago in Tokyo. They felt that the time had come for Khaliq to avenge his defeat. While the two of us were going through our warm-up exercises, there were deafening shouts from all the spectators: 'Long Live Pakistan, Long Live Abdul Khaliq.' The entire audience kept cheering for him as he walked in before me, followed by other Pakistani athletes and Makhan Singh, the only other Indian besides me.

At the starting line, I put down my bag, warmed-up and

wiped the perspiration from my body with a towel. As we waited for the race to begin, a couple of moulvis, with flowing beards, skullcaps and carrying rosaries in their hands, encircled Khaliq. They blessed him, saying, 'May Allah be with you.' Irritated by this blatant favouritism, I shouted, 'Moulvi Sahib, we, too, are the children of the same God. Don't we deserve the same blessings?' For a moment, they were dumbstruck, and then one of them half-heartedly muttered, 'May God strengthen your legs, too.'

There was pin-drop silence as we stood at the starting line waiting for the race to begin. The silence was oppressive. The starter, dressed in a white shirt and trousers, a red overall, white peaked cap and black shoes, stood on a table behind us. He shouted, 'On your marks,' fired the gun and the race began. The audience suddenly awoke and began to chant: 'Pakistan zindabad; Abdul Khaliq zindabad.' Khaliq was ahead of me but I caught up before we had completed the first 100 metres. We were shoulder-to-shoulder, then surprisingly, Khaliq seemed to slacken and I surged ahead as if on wings. I finished the 200 metres about ten yards ahead of Khaliq, clocking 20.7 seconds that equalled the world record. My coach, Ranbir Singh, the manager and all my team members leapt to their feet in jubilation. I was embraced, thumped on the back and then lifted on to their shoulders as they expressed their happiness both vocally and physically.

It was indeed a joyful day for India, but a terrible tragedy for Pakistan. Khaliq himself was so devastated that he lay on the ground weeping pitifully. I patted his back and tried to console him by saying that victory and defeat were part of the same game and should not be taken to heart, but he was too humiliated by the fact that he had been defeated before the eyes of his countrymen.

After the race, I ran a victory lap of the stadium, while loudspeakers announced: 'The athlete running before you is Milkha Singh. He does not run, he flies! His victory will be recorded in Pakistan's sports' history, and we confer the title of "Flying Sikh" on him.' It was General Ayub Khan who coined the title 'Flying Sikh', when he had congratulated me, saying, '*Tum daude nahi, udhey ho*—you do not run, but fly!' As I passed in front of the women's section, the ladies lifted their burqas from their faces so that they could have a closer look at me—an incident that was widely reported in the Pakistani press.

And so, with this victory, I became the Flying Sikh, a title that soon became synonymous with my name all over the world.

12
Going West

I returned to India in a thoughtful mood. I had confronted my past while in Pakistan and accepted the reality that I was the product of both countries—Pakistan was my childhood where I had learnt how to face hardships, India was my youth and adulthood that saw the fulfilment of my dreams.

After a few days in Delhi, I left for Germany as captain of India's athletic team. This was the first stop on a tour of Europe that extended from May to July 1960 and culminated with the Rome Olympics in August.

I was pleasantly surprised to discover how famous I was in Germany. My first race in Frankfurt was a friendly contest where I would be participating with one of their top athletes, Carl Kaufmann. When I was introduced to this splendid young man who later became a good friend of mine, he shyly told me, through an interpreter, that his countrymen believed that except for Milkha Singh, he had no equals in the world.

Typically, I was not in the best of spirits on the day of the contest. Perhaps I was still jet-lagged or had yet to get acclimatized to the weather. As a result, I lost the first race badly. My coach, Ranbir Singh, and teammates tried very hard to console me, but I was too humiliated by my defeat. I had never lost a 400-metre race till that day, so how could this happen?

Another contest was held at Cologne a few days later. I performed better this time and Kaufmann and I were tied for the first place. For me, this was as bad as being defeated. Then, it was announced that as a result of a photo finish, I had reached the tape before Kaufmann. My victory convinced Kaufmann that I was getting back into form and that it would be more prudent to avoid further contests. Another German ace sprinter, Manfred Kinder, participated in several races with me, but I won each of them.

We spent about fifteen or twenty days in Germany, and one amusing incident still stands out. On the day we arrived in Cologne, one of our team members, Lal Chand, champion of the 26-mile marathon, was the cause of much hilarity. The team was staying in a high-rise hotel and had been allocated rooms on different floors. When we reached the hotel, we were told to deposit our luggage in our respective rooms and then assemble in the dining room on the ground floor. Being familiar with the mechanics of how a lift worked, we reached our destination without any mishap. But not Lal Chand, a simple-minded fellow ignorant of new technology, who went up and down for thirty minutes, without knowing how to get off. Each time he tried to step out of the lift the doors would close on him. When the other passengers enquired which floor he wanted, he did not understand what they were saying, and just smiled. Finally, he landed on the ground floor, wearing no necktie or shoes, just his bathroom slippers. He looked dishevelled and harassed and complained loudly that he been caught in the clutches of a demonic contraption that refused to let him go! We were embarrassed by his appearance and the attention he was attracting from the other diners and immediately dispatched him to his room, telling him that he must return properly dressed for dinner. But he lost his bearings, again. After dinner I went to Lal Chand's room to find out what had happened and found him arguing with the hotel staff. Apparently, his shoes and suitcase were missing from his room. I tried to reason with him, explaining that this was a five-star hotel with a reputation to uphold, and that his baggage could not have been stolen; it must have been misplaced and would be returned to him. But my words had no effect on him and he marched out of the room.

His next target was the receptionist, who could not understand what he was saying, but was eager to help a guest. She sent a couple of attendants up to his room, and when they entered, he pointed towards his bare feet to indicate that he had could not find his shoes. Misunderstanding him, they took him to a shoe shop where he raised a ruckus again, saying that he didn't want new shoes, he wanted his own ones back. When he returned to his room, he explained the situation to me in Punjabi and I communicated the problem of his missing clothes to the interpreter in English. It was then that we discovered that he had left his room in such a mess that the staff had helpfully tidied up after him—his shoes had been placed under the telephone table, and his clothes had been ironed and packed inside his suitcase. Much ado about nothing! Lal Chand had spent three hours caught up in a whirlwind of his own making, and to top it all, had missed his dinner as well.

I have always had a special love for Germany and the German people. Over the years, I have been back several times, visiting many cities, including Frankfurt, Cologne, Munich and even Berlin during the Cold War years. When I saw the Berlin Wall, I was deeply saddened to see how one nation had been forcibly split into two by this forbidding artificial boundary. It was yet another instance of how the lives of ordinary citizens are disturbed by politics. The Germans were familiar with my records and achievements and admired me to such an extent that they even had calendars printed with my photograph.

From Germany we flew to London, and then on to the British army base at Aldershot, about 140 miles away, where we had to undergo a military training course. We were put up in the barracks, while our manager, a naval officer called Commander Pereira, stayed at the officers' quarters nearby. We had brought along a cook from India, Harnam Singh, who had once been employed by the Maharaja of Patiala. We had also carried dry provisions like flour, pulses and masalas, and would go to the market every day to buy fresh vegetables, meat or chicken so that Harnam could prepare desi-style khana for us. None of us could have survived on bland English food.

One day, I received a visit from a distraught Englishman who lived on the military base. He had a peculiar problem that he wanted to share with me, which involved the Indian 32-mile walking champion, Zora Singh. The champion had a flourishing six-inch-long handlebar moustache, whose tips almost reached up to his eyes. Apparently, when Zora walked past their house, his appearance so terrified the English officer's three-year-old son that he would shriek in fear. Zora Singh, oblivious of the impact he had, tried to be friendly, but the child was too traumatized to be pacified. Our team was highly amused by the incident and persuaded Zora Singh to either avoid interacting with the child or trim his moustache. He decided to trim it; after all, he could always grow it back again once we returned to India.

Behind the barracks there was a large, beautifully maintained playing field, where we would practice every morning and evening. Our next event, was an important athletic contest in London, in which sportsmen from fifty countries would be participating. London's Punjabi community had turned up in full force and cheered me vociferously when I won race after race. The English gardener at the stadium was a fan of mine and would always wish me good luck before a race. 'Mr Singh, I want to see you win,' he would say, jumping up and down. After each win, I would give him a small tip.

While I was in England, I had received a special invitation

from the Soviet Union to participate in a race in Moscow. This event was held in memory of the Znamensky brothers, Georgy and Seraphim, who, in the 1930s, were the Soviet long-distance champions. This tournament, first established in 1958, is today an annual event that draws athletes from all over the world. But when I went there in 1960, most of the participants were from Soviet Bloc countries, though there were a few sportspeople from Asia and Europe, including Korea, France, Norway and England.

That was also the era when the India–Russia Friendship Treaty was at its strongest, and wherever we went we would be greeted by cries of 'Rusi–Hindi bhai, bhai', and snatches of Hindi film songs. Raj Kapoor and Nargis were probably more popular in the Soviet Union then they were in India. Their film *Awara* had been released in 1951 and since then its actors were treated like glamorous celebrities. The Russian people had tremendous admiration for our country and I was astonished by how much they knew about our history, particularly the freedom movement and Independence, and leaders like Mahatma Gandhi and Nehru.

Nina, my English-speaking interpreter, was equally curious about India, and would keep asking me questions about the conditions of our workers and peasants. I was pleasantly surprised by the serious tone of her enquiries. Most other foreigners I had met seemed more interested in the more exotic aspects of India—elephants, maharajas, snake charmers, jugglers and mendicants. That's when it dawned upon me how different the Soviet Union was from Western countries.

Whenever I entered the Lenin Stadium, young boys and girls would run up to Nina, requesting her to get them my autograph, or asking me, through her, to tell them the story of my life and career. While listening to their eager questions, I contemplated on the meaning of fame. Adulation and glory can be a double-edged sword that can make or break a celebrity. In the world of sports, fans follow and cheer their favourites, particularly when they win and break records, but the moment their hero falters, their allegiance moves to the next rising star.

In this meet, too, my win was the result of a photo finish, the camera proving that it was my torso that hit the finishing tape first. The crowds were overjoyed, particularly the sizable Indian population that was living in Moscow, who leapt out of their seats and ran into the stadium, embracing me and lifting me up on to their shoulders with excitement.

I was interviewed by the Soviet press agencies, which asked me a series of searching questions: What were my impressions about the Soviet Union? What did I think of Indo-Soviet relations? What did the people of India think of Russia? They seemed to be fairly happy with my bland replies.

When I left Moscow for London, Nina and a few others came to the airport to see me off. I had made some good friends during my short time in the city. I continued to keep in touch with them for a while, and today, when I read their letters, I remember the good times we had together all those years ago. For years I had corresponded with many other friends, admirers, and even strangers, who had entered my life at some time or the other. For me, meeting new people, befriending them and then parting was a normal part of the interactions I've had with a large number of strangers over the years. Yet, for me, establishing contact with my fans was of the greatest importance.

13

So Near, and Yet So Far

A month before the Rome Olympics, the preliminaries were held in London. While sitting in the gallery watching the races, I observed the black French athlete, Abdul Saye, clock an unbelievable 45.9 seconds in the 400-metre event. This was a sensational record and was most worrying because my timing in the same race was a little over 46 seconds. When the French heard that Milkha Singh was part of the Indian Olympic team they invited me to France for the next preliminaries in which reputed sprinters from England, Jamaica, the West Indies and Kenya were participating. This was just a week or so before the Olympics.

My track record before this event had been impeccable. I had run many races and won against other world-class athletes, but Abdul Saye was a challenge. Usually I had beaten other contestants by a margin of five or seven yards, but could I do the same this time? Commander Pereira, in his broken Hindustani, did his best to motivate me, saying, 'Milkha Singh, you must beat Abdul Saye today.'

In the stadium, the mostly French audience watched as I went through my warm-up exercises. To them, I was a curiosity with my long hair, turban and kara and they did not know what to expect of me. When the race began, I ran with a vengeance, straining every muscle and won, establishing a new record of 45.8 seconds—point one second less than the previous Olympic record of 45.9. My achievement made headline news in the international press the next day. When I returned to my hotel room, I watched the reruns of the race that were being telecast on television. It was a new experience to watch myself run as well as observe the audience's reaction to my win. I was deeply gratified by the accolades I had received.

When I returned to Aldershot, my team members were elated by my victory and were convinced that I would have the same success in Rome.

Rome, the Eternal City, looked very festive when the Indian contingent, led by Ashwini Kumar, landed at the airport. Milling crowds filled streets lined with flags and banners. As we drove through this historic city towards the Olympic Village, we were infected by the excitement around us. This time, I was privileged enough to be given a separate room so that I would not be disturbed by too many visitors.

Rome in August is hot, almost like India. On the opening day the temperatures had risen to above 40 degrees Celsius and it was extremely uncomfortable. Yet, the crowds were not daunted by the weather and filled the stands by the thousands, carrying red and black umbrellas as protection against the sun. The mammoth stadium, Stadio Olimpica, had been recently renovated and looked very impressive. The opening ceremony was spectacular. The military bands played the Italian national anthem and marches from operas, including Bellini's *Norma* and Verdi's *Ernani*, as the smartly dressed contingents from all over the world saluted the president of Italy, Giovanni Gronchi, when they briskly marched past his box. And as the Olympic flag was being raised, a choir sang the anthem of the Games with great emotion.

Athletes from almost a hundred and fifty nations were participating in the 400-metre race. I won round after round in every heat until I reached the semi-finals. By now only twelve of us remained, but in this race the number would be further reduced to the top six. The semi-finals took place and I was through to the final.

Over the years, I had, through continuous hard work and an intense practice schedule, built up my stamina to such a high level that I could compete in and often win two races each day, even in global competitions. Sadly, this ability was of little consequence in Rome, mainly because of the curious two-night gap between the semis and the finals. As a result I had more time to think and brood. I was so nervous and tense that I spent two sleepless nights before the finals. The night before, I kept thinking about the race and that put me under a lot of pressure. I was extremely tense and paced the floor in agitation, wondering what the next day would have in store for me. Then there was a knock on my door. It was Mr Umrao Singh, our manager, who came in and whisked me off for a long walk. As we wandered through the cobbled streets, past noble edifices, fountains and archways, he tried to distract me from the forthcoming contest by talking about the Punjab and telling me stirring stories of the Sikh Gurus and other valiant heroes. We walked and talked, and for a while I was at peace.

Early next morning, I returned to the stadium and joined the other participants at the starting line. It was at the moment when the lanes were being allocated that everything went wrong. Carl Kaufmann was in the first lane, the American Ottis Davis in the second, while the third one went to a participant from Poland and the fourth to my old Commonwealth Games' rival, Malcolm Spence. I had the misfortune to be given the fifth lane next to a German athlete, who was the weakest of the six of us. This was a huge blow to me because the German was the only runner in my line of vision. With nothing but negative thoughts running through my mind, I took my standing position. When the starter shouted, 'On your marks!' I got down on my knees and offered a silent prayer to the ground beneath me, 'Oh, Mother Earth, you have bestowed many favours on me. I pray that you will do the same today.' I bowed my head and took a deep breath. The starter shouted

'Set!' and when he fired his gun we flew off at lightning speed.

I started off by being ahead of the others, and at the 250-metre mark, I was running so perilously fast that I decided to slow down in case I collapsed—a fatal decision I regret even to this day. As I completed 300 metres, the three competitors right behind me came abreast and began to move ahead, and even though I increased my speed, trying desperately to catch up with Spence, who I had beaten at Cardiff, or the two before him, I could not wipe out the deficit of those six or seven yards. And thus, as fate would have it, my error of judgment at that crucial point in the race, had dragged me to the fourth position and destroyed all my chances of winning that elusive Olympic gold.

Yet, it was a very close race, where the top positions were decided through a photo finish, which meant that the announcements were delayed. The suspense was excruciating. When the results were declared, all four of us—Davis, Kaufmann, Spence and I—had shattered the previous Olympic record of 45.9 seconds. Davis had come first with 44.9 seconds; Kaufmann was second with the same time of 44.9 seconds and Spence third with 45.5 seconds. Even though I had come fourth, my timing of 45.6 seconds was still a new record.

I felt completely bereft and humiliated by what had happened. I had scaled the heights of success and now the decline had set in. I knew no one can remain on the top forever. I had dominated the global sports scene for several years and it was time to go. I felt that I could not return to India in this dejected frame of mind, and so participated in competitions in London, Denmark, Sweden and Norway. And then it was time to get back home. On the flight back, I drank copiously to drown my sorrow and landed in Bombay in an inebriated condition, tired and filled with self-loathing. This time, however, there were no adoring crowds waiting eagerly to welcome me, just a few members of the press. Several well-wishers tried to console me, saying that one loss was not the end of the world and that other prestigious awards awaited me, but I remained adamant that my days as a sportsman were over.

Next day, my retirement was headline news. Many fans and supporters sent letters of regret, begging me to re-consider my decision. They said that Milkha Singh was not an ordinary individual, but the custodian of India's honour in the sports world, and that I must continue to run, not for private gain, but for the glory of my country. Despite the defeat, I was still the hope of Indian athletes, they insisted. Thus, goaded by pressure from the press and sports officials, and the support of friends I rescinded my decision. After a short period of 'mourning', I resumed my practice again.

All through my life, I have been tormented by the fatal mistake I made in Rome on the day of the 400-metre race. I knew that I could have won, but perhaps, luck was not on my side that day. The one medal I had yearned for throughout my career had just slipped through my fingers because of one small error of judgement. Even today, if I look back on my life, there are only two incidents that still haunt me—the massacre of my family during Partition and my defeat at Rome.

14

From Sports to Administration

In 1959, Gurnam Singh Tir, the Punjab government's public relations officer, had kindly fixed an appointment for me with the chief minister of Punjab, Sardar Pratap Singh Kairon, who was a towering political figure in Punjab and wielded immense power at the state as well as national level. The little I knew about him was what I had gleaned from newspapers, but as a sportsman I had little understanding about the nature of politics and the extent of influence a politician commands. In our meeting, Kairon asked me probing questions about the state of Indian sports and why our athletes performed so poorly in the international arena, unlike their counterparts from other countries who won large numbers of gold and silver medals. What did their training involve? Did their governments actively support their endeavours? Give them financial aid and special benefits? He strongly believed that Indians, too, had the potential to succeed, but lacked the opportunities to develop their talents and skills. He then outlined his proposal of setting up a separate department of sports under the auspices of the Punjab government where fit young Punjabi boys could be trained under my charge.

What the chief minister was suggesting was that I leave the army and take on a civilian post. He then started to negotiate terms, comparing my current salary of seventy rupees a month with the remuneration he was offering of eight or twelve hundred rupees. Not only was this extremely generous, it would also elevate me to a general's grade. It did seem promising, but I was sceptical about the outcome. I knew Kairon had tremendous clout, but could he actually procure such a prestigious position for me? My friends and colleagues thought I was crazy to leave the army as they all felt that civilian jobs were not permanent and dependent upon the whims and fancies of politicians. More important, I had heard that an order had been sent to the defence minister, Krishna Menon, recommending that I be promoted to the rank of lieutenant. This was a great honour for me and meant that I, who joined as a humble jawan, would soon be a commissioned officer. This news added to my confusion.

My noncommittal response to his proposal had no effect on Kairon Sahib, and he continued to woo me. Whenever he was in Delhi, he used to stay at the Constitution Club near the National Stadium, where I would be practising. He would send regular emissaries to persuade me to change my mind. When I met Kairon Sahib again after I returned from Rome in 1960, I expressed my doubts about getting an honourable discharge from military service, but he airily dismissed these away. He emphasized that he would take care of all the formalities if I accepted his offer. He also assured me that all my requests would be granted without questions.

A few days later, Kairon took me along to a function at Parliament House. The high-powered guest list included the prime minister, union ministers, chief ministers and other high-ranking dignitaries. When we arrived at Parliament House, there was much jubilation among the assembled guests that Milkha Singh had arrived, but little did I (or anyone else) know why I was there. It was Kairon's intention to bring up my case before Pandit Nehru so that a decision could be taken then and there. He outlined his plan of setting up a sports department in Chandigarh to train promising young boys and girls. He said that for his plan to succeed, he needed an experienced and highly celebrated athlete like me to take charge of the programme. Therefore, he requested that the prime minister permit my discharge so that I could take up my position with the Punjab government as soon as possible.

Panditji was reluctant to make a quick decision, knowing that my resignation would be a big blow to the army under whose benign patronage I had grown and triumphed as a sportsman. But Kairon Sahib was so persistent that Panditji had no option but to inform Krishna Menon and General Thimayya that they should relieve me of my duties so that I was free to enter the service of the Punjab government. He added, tongue-in-cheek, 'Milkha Singh is an Indian, so what difference does it make if he's in the army or with the Punjab government? We will all share the honour he brings. Besides, in any case, he has given up running races.' Hearing this, Krishna Menon burst out laughing, but General Thimayya was not amused, though there was little he could do to circumvent a decision that had been taken at the highest level. He took me aside and embracing me said, 'Young man, you are just like a son to me, you are making a terrible mistake. A civilian job is shaky, unlike the army where your career is assured. Besides, in a few days, we will be promoting you to lieutenant. I hope you will not regret this step.'

The die had been cast, however, and the next day a telegram was sent to my unit in Secunderabad, ordering them to prepare all the necessary papers for my discharge. My centre commander, Colonel Barve, was thunderstruck when he received that fateful telegram, and sadly broke the news to the other officers and jawans.

The unit had been home to me ever since I had joined as a raw recruit in 1953. It was the only family I knew, who had loved, nurtured and guided me through all the vicissitudes of life, encouraging and supporting me to fulfil my dream of being a world-class athlete. And now it was time to say goodbye, to leave my safe haven and enter a new, unfamiliar world.

It was a sad and poignant farewell. Colonel Barve addressed a huge assembly of sorrowful jawans and officers, saying that although he was deeply distressed by my decision to leave both the army and unit, he nevertheless would like to wish me good luck in my future endeavours. When it was my turn to speak, I could not find the words to express the heartfelt love and gratitude I felt for the people who stood before me. I only knew that I would never forget my unit and my colleagues and all the years I spent there. I recalled the tough life in the barracks, the early morning roll calls and hard labour, the hours I spent on the playing fields, the rigorous training schedule I had forced myself to endure, and all the kindness I had received from my officers, coaches and fellow soldiers. It was because of their confidence in me that I had risen from a nonentity to a celebrity. I ended my speech by appealing to Colonel Barve to produce many more Milkha Singhs, so that our unit could keep this tradition alive.

I was overwhelmed by the warmth of their affection, and by the generous gifts I received—a silver glass, silver thali, a beautiful embossed salver and a gold kara that I still treasure along with my memories of the EME Centre. But the transition was complete—my life in the army had ended and a new one as a civilian awaited me.

I spent the next four months on a well-deserved holiday. Yet, I was still concerned about the nature of my job. The salary that Kairon Sahib had offered was more than double the amount I was getting in the army. And though the thought of earning more money pleased me, I was not so sure what the work involved. After all, I was a sportsman not an administrator. What did I know about a desk job?

When I joined the sports department in November 1961, I discovered that a post had been specially created for me, that of deputy director of sports. My first few weeks there, however, were a struggle and there were times when I deeply regretted my decision to leave the army. Initially, I had to commute from Delhi to Chandigarh and back again each day. I would leave Delhi at about 4 a.m. to reach office by 9, and then, after a long day, would jump into my car at 5 p.m. so that I could be home by 9.30 p.m. It was long and tedious journey, and invariably I would report to work much past the stipulated time.

I used to drive a Fiat. In those days, people had to wait for months to buy cars and scooters. But because I was 'India's best athlete', Lal Bahadur Shastri, who was transport minister then, kindly allocated an 'out-of-turn delivery' for me. I had bought the car for five thousand rupees in 1958 with the help of money I had won as an incentive. I was at the Tokyo Asiad, when the Maharaja of Patiala, Yadavindra Singh, challenged me, saying, 'If you beat Abdul Khaliq in the 200-metre race, I will give you five thousand rupees.' I did, and that is how I had the money to purchase my first car—earlier I used to ride a motorcycle.

But being India's best athlete made little difference to my working life in Chandigarh. My irregular timings had led to tension in the office, and I found it difficult to cope with the constant reprimands. More important, my long commute as well as trying to adjust to a sedentary lifestyle had left me with little time to practice, a routine that I could not afford to miss, particularly since the next event was the Jakarta Asian Games in 1962.

In frustration, I went to Kairon Sahib and complained that I was not enjoying spending my entire day doing paperwork and other administrative duties, when I should be out on the track practising. If I were still in the army I would have been exempted from military duties and allowed to spend as much time as I could on the field, practising. The chief minister severely reprimanded my senior officer. He told him that Milkha Singh was our nation's pride and should not be restricted to the mundane routine of office work. Instead, he should be allowed the freedom to attend office as and when he could; that his priority was to run for the country.

As a result of that meeting, I was given accommodation in Chandigarh, and my office hours were relaxed. I was able to resume my morning and evening practice routine. Over time, I also began to get more involved with my sports development work and started enjoying creating projects that were close to my heart.

At the same time, I continued to participate in events in India as well as overseas. I was part of the Indian contingent for the Jakarta Asian Games in August 1962, where I won two gold medals, one for the 400-metre race and the other as part of the 4x400-metre relay team. And then it was on to the Olympics in Tokyo in 1964, after which I hung up my boots. My sports career finally set in 1964. A new chapter now awaited me.

Soon after retiring, I announced that I would give an award of two lakh rupees to any athlete who broke my record of

45.6 seconds in the Olympics. So far, this has not happened, but I have stipulated that whenever it happens, my son Jeev will honour the award.

15
Nimmi

I first met Nimmi in 1956 in Colombo.

I was in Ceylon (now Sri Lanka) to participate in an athletic competition, and she was there in her capacity as captain of the Indian women's volleyball team to play a friendly match against the Ceylonese. One day, while my friends and I were wandering around the bazaar, we came across a group of Indian girls and Nimmi was among them. As it always happens, when Indians, or for that matter any other nationalities, meet their fellow countrymen in an alien land, there is instant recognition and bonds of camaraderie are forged based on language, culture and traditions, even if they are total strangers. Inevitably, we struck up a conversation with them, and Nimmi insisted that I come to watch their match that evening. Naturally, I did not refuse, if for no other reason than to support her team.

I reached the venue two hours ahead of the scheduled time, full of anticipation. The Indian team was in full form, but Nimmi's performance was outstanding—her electric energy, superb high jumps and how she ran up to the net to hit the ball. It appeared as if she could beat the entire Ceylonese team single-handedly on their home ground. Her skills were admirable.

I was eager to meet Nimmi again, but needed a valid excuse. I suggested to my friend, tea magnate Daljit Singh Sitara, that he host a reception at his residence in Ceylon for the victorious Indian volleyball team. His invitation was accepted and the dinner party was fixed for the next evening, after my race. The girls had demanded entry passes for my competition and turned up in full force for the event. I ran as one possessed, very much aware of Nimmi's presence. There was absolutely no question of me losing the race, not with Nimmi as an onlooker. I wanted to impress her and it would just be too humiliating if I lost. When I won, I stood before Nimmi and was thrilled by the glow of happiness on her face.

At the dinner party, Nimmi discussed my race in minute detail, and I was struck by how interested she was in my life and career. It seemed obvious that we were on the brink of a new relationship, and I was determined to see her again, but we were at a party and I had no card or piece of paper to write down my telephone number. So quietly, lest anyone could see, I caught hold of her hand and quickly wrote the number down on her palm. My touch made her blush and she nervously looked around, wiping the sweat from her brow with her dupatta. The rush of emotions that swept across me electrified me and I couldn't sleep a wink that night. The next morning, before she left for India, Nimmi telephoned me and we agreed to meet at the Yadavindra Stadium in Patiala, where I practised regularly, when I was with my unit there.

When I returned to Patiala from Colombo two days later, I received a telephone call from the principal of the College of Physical Education, who informed me that some of his students, including Nimmi, were coming to watch me practice. She had wisely taken this precaution in case our growing relationship would lead to gossip. When I met the principal, I congratulated him on the volleyball team's victory in Colombo and made special mention of Nimmi's contribution.

Nimmi and I met a couple of times thereafter, while we were both practising at the stadium—she volleyball and I running. But there were few outward signs that our relationship was ripening into love. All it amounted to, at that stage, was a strong attraction between two people of the opposite sex. We shared a bond, but for that bond to grow, we needed time, which was not possible, mainly because my calendar was packed with events that made it impossible for me to stay in one place for any length of time. After a few days I had to hurriedly leave Patiala and had no time to inform Nimmi of my departure. I must sadly admit that my travels and the numerous events that I was competing in soon obliterated all thoughts of Nimmi.

It was during this period of my life that I, too, had begun

to experience the adulation and admiration that popular film stars and other celebrities face. My career and fame were on the rise, and I remember all the lovely ladies I had encountered when I participated in running events across Europe, Asia, and even India, who cheered loudly and clustered around me, asking for autographs or just gazing at me with adoring eyes. I still remember Betty, Australia's sprint queen whom I met at the Melbourne Olympics in 1956. She had never seen a sardar before and was mesmerized by my turban. I taught her how to tie it and even presented her with one of mine. To be honest, I could have succumbed to temptation, but then I would always recall my vow of abstinence, well aware of the deleterious effect sex would have on my mind and body. Sex can play havoc with the self-imposed discipline and practice routine that is so essential for an athlete's growth and development.

Although my sister, Isher, was very keen to arrange a marriage for me, I was really not interested at that stage, simply because I could never find a girl who could measure up to my all-absorbing devotion to sports, or for whose love I could sacrifice my métier, my chosen goal.

When I returned from the Tokyo Asian Games in 1958, the principal of the College of Physical Education in Patiala invited me to give his students a lecture on the Asian Games. I had little experience of public speaking, but agreed even though I thought it incongruous that a young man like myself should be addressing an audience who were almost the same age.

When I took my place at the podium, I began by thanking the principal for the honour he had extended to me by inviting me to address his students. I then narrated some of the highlights of the races I had participated in. Girls were seated in the front row of the auditorium while boys filled the benches behind them. It was here that I saw Nirmal, or Nimmi as she was affectionately called, again. She was talking animatedly to her friends, and I presumed somehow that I was the subject of her witty comments. After my lecture, several girls and boys came up to me for autographs or to be photographed with me, but Nimmi remained aloof. Perhaps she was too shy, or too proud to join the crowd. I saw her staring at me but lacked the courage to single her out for a chat so that we could renew our acquaintance.

There had been an innocence in my experience with the fairer sex so far, but I soon realized how convoluted the mating game could be. It was at an exhibition on Mathura Road in Delhi when I first set eyes on one of the most striking young ladies I had ever seen. As a joke, a friend said, 'Milkha, do you think you could attract this girl?' We joked about it and left it there. As it transpired, she and her mother came to watch me run at the All-India Athletic Meet at the National Stadium the following day. When I won the race, she came up to congratulate me and generously invited my friends and me for dinner at her house. That evening my friends teased me mercilessly, saying, 'Beware, the loveliest rose has thorns that can scratch you.'

The next day we went to her palatial house for dinner and met her parents, who welcomed me warmly like a son, indicating that they had no objection to their daughter's friendship with me. They were an affluent business family and they shrewdly felt that having a famous sportsman as a son-in-law would be good publicity for their company. As our interactions increased, I began to feel very uneasy and stifled by the way her parents took command of my life and how they tried to control my every move, to the extent that whenever I returned from an overseas trip, their car would be waiting for me at Palam airport and they would whisk me off to their house. They even tried to interfere with my future, and dismissed my dreams and aspirations; instead they wanted me to focus on how my image could enhance their business.

She entered my life when I was young and impressionable, and it was clear to me, right from the start, that we could never have forged a deeper relationship. She was very beautiful and we were close friends, but I had no desire to give in to her family's demands and diktats.

Gradually, I began to distance myself from the family, but they were extremely influential and threatened that if I did not marry their daughter, they would destroy my career, or even get me murdered. Their threats and warnings, however, did not frighten me. By now I had moved to Chandigarh and hoped that the matter would be forgotten.

There were times when I would miss having a soulmate in my life, but I did not want to lose focus in my quest to become the best athlete in the world.

🏃

Keeping fit, 1958

With coach, Dr Howard,
before the Cardiff Commonwealth Games, 1958

Tumbling over the finishing line to win the 200-metre race,
Tokyo Asiad 1958

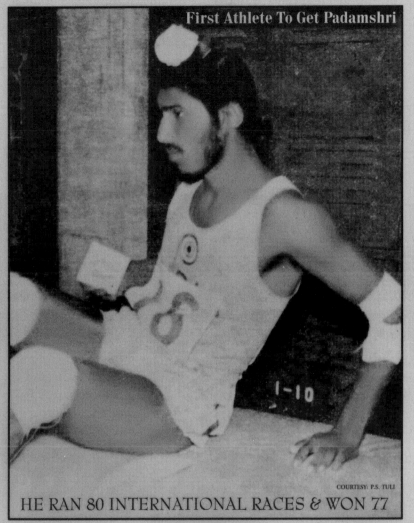

INDIA'S HIGHEST DECORATED & CELEBRATED ATHLETE

First Athlete To Get Padamshri

COURTESY: P.S. TULI

HE RAN 80 INTERNATIONAL RACES & WON 77

Milkha Singh, The" Flying Sikh" won India's FIRST Gold Medal ever at the British Empire & Commonwealth Games In 1958 (Cardiff)

After having pulled a muscle in the 200-metre race, Tokyo Asiad 1958

Asia's Best Athlete, Tokyo Asiad 1958

A hero's welcome, with Parduman Singh, Patiala 1958

The proud JCO (junior commissioned officer) with Pandit Nehru, 1958

With my EME commanding officer,
Brigadier SP Vohra, Secunderabad, 1958

Winning the gold at the Cardiff Commonwealth Games, 1958

The Dancing Sardar

Cologne, Germany 1960, with (from left to right): Mohinder Singh, Milkha Singh, Makhan Singh, Daljit Singh

With India's standard, Jakarta Asian Games, 1962

Nimmi with friends/with the volleyball team

The coy bride, 5 May 1963

We are man and wife, Anand Karaj ceremony, 5 May 1963

With Dhyan Chand and Dara Singh

My sister, Isher Kaur

Holidaying with the family (from left to right): Jeev, Aleeza, Milkha, Mona, Nimmi, Sonia,

The keen sikhari

To the manor born

With former prime minister, Indira Gandhi

With former President, Giani Zail Singh, and Yadavindra Singh, the Maharaja of Patiala

Handing over the Peace Torch

Spreading friendship, with a Masai warrior, Kenya

Jeev in action

16

The Bird and a Melancholic Tree

Around the same time, in 1960, I unexpectedly met Nimmi again. At that time, she was working as the DPE (deputy physical education) instructor at Delhi's Lady Irwin College. One day, while I was practising at the stadium, I was invited to attend a volleyball match, and when I entered the enclosure, there was an announcement saying: 'It is a matter of great pride for us that Milkha Singh, the Flying Sikh, has graced this competition with his presence.' All eyes turned towards me, and deeply embarrassed, I quietly took my seat. Soon after the match was over, a young lady came up to me, folded her hands and greeted me with 'Sat Sri Akal'.

I looked up and recognized Nimmi immediately. But what a transformation! Nimmi as a student displayed all the mannerisms of a frivolous adolescent and was always demurely dressed in a salwar–kameez and dupatta with her long hair tied in two plaits. Today, wearing a sari and her hair knotted in a bun, she had the poise and confidence of a professional young lady. I couldn't reconcile the two disparate images.

After the competition, she came up to me and insisted that I accompany her for tea in her hostel, which was fairly close to the stadium. While we talked, my old feelings for her returned, much stronger now than ever before. How could I have forgotten such a beautiful and empathetic young woman? She reproached me, saying, ' You are like a carefree bird moving from tree to tree, while I am like that melancholic tree, upon which you alighted for a brief moment and then flew off. Have you ever once thought of this miserable tree who finds herself alone and abandoned?'

After a few minutes of silence, I said, 'I have no reply to your question, Nimmi.'

But from that day onwards, our relationship changed and we began to meet more often. This was also the period when my professional life had entered a new chapter. I had resigned from the army and was now based in Chandigarh, a city that had been constructed as recently as the 1950s. It was a sprawling, sparsely populated place and I felt unsettled and lonely without my friends and colleagues. And though I missed them, I missed Nimmi even more, and would drive to Delhi every weekend to spend time with her.

One evening, I picked Nimmi up from her hostel and took her for a drive in my Fiat down Mathura Road. We were so engrossed in our conversation that we hadn't realized that the car had hit the pavement and ploughed through a group of labourers, injuring one of the women. The crowd that had collected shouted at me and smashed the car's window frames in rage. I tried to placate them, but their mood was ugly and I was soon surrounded by an angry mob. Nimmi was watching the proceedings with growing anxiety, fearful that because of the accident our clandestine meetings would be publicized and her family and the college authorities would come to hear of them. Some of the onlookers recognized me and appeared sympathetic, and in desperation, I appealed to them to take Nimmi back to her college. She didn't want to leave me, but I insisted. I then turned my attention towards the injured woman, put her gently into the car and took her to the nearest hospital. I paid for the woman's fractured leg to be X-rayed and for the subsequent treatment and also gave her husband one month's salary ex gratia. I felt this was the least I could have done.

We continued to meet in Delhi while Nimmi was still at Lady Irwin College, but she soon took up a position as assistant director at the Sports Department, Punjab, where I was deputy director. This gave us a chance to meet more often, both in the office during our lunch and tea breaks and in the evenings when we would take long walks along the lake. However, unlike a bustling metropolis like Delhi, Chandigarh was a small town and our regular meetings did not go unnoticed. People began to talk and word of our relationship soon reached the ears of our all-powerful chief minister, which displeased him greatly. There was another added complication that made Kairon Sahib even angrier. The affluent Delhi family had heard about my courtship of Nimmi, and wrote furious letters to Kairon Sahib, denouncing me for my callous treatment of their daughter. Goaded by the onslaught of their letters, the chief minister called for me and demanded to know what was going on.

I narrated the truth about what took place in Delhi, explaining that there was nothing untoward in my friendship with the girl; we would meet for the occasional cup of coffee, or just for a chat. I added that if he and her family didn't believe me they could check with the girl.

He shot back, 'Your intimacy with Nirmal has become a public scandal. This is very bad.'

I humbly said to him, 'Sir, if you are displeased with me I will resign and leave Chandigarh. But first, I request you to give me a fair and patient hearing.' I then proceeded to tell him that I loved Nimmi and wanted to marry her.

He listened sympathetically, and said, 'If you want to marry Nirmal, go ahead at once. Otherwise stop meeting her.'

I was overjoyed that the chief minister had believed me and had given his consent to our marriage. But what I didn't expect, and what I should have, was how difficult it was to break the social conventions of those days. In the 1960s, inter-caste marriages were frowned upon, and my family vehemently declared that under no circumstances would they agree to their brother marrying a Hindu.

By now the news of our relationship had reached Nimmi's

parents, and they were furious. Her father, Choudhury Mehar Chand Saini, was an influential man and a staunch Arya Samaji, and he was convinced that if his daughter married a Sikh his reputation and izzat would be at stake. Besides, they had been trying to fix a match for her with an eligible engineer who had just returned from Canada. They demanded that Nimmi return home to Pathankot immediately and attempted to brainwash her to accept the proposal.

When Nimmi returned to Chandigarh, she was deeply distressed and wept in my arms. Would family pressure force us to part? Was this the end of our romantic dreams? Despite her sorrow, Nimmi found the courage to confront her mother with an ultimatum—either to allow her to marry Milkha Singh or she would remain a spinster all her life. But her threats made no difference to their opposition.

Finally, Kairon Sahib decided to step in and break the impasse. He spoke to Nimmi's father, whom he knew very well, at great length, convincing him to agree to the match. He explained that both Nimmi and I were determined to marry each other, and if her family continued to object, what would prevent her from eloping and having a court marriage? We both were of age, so we did not need parental consent. 'Wouldn't such a step,' he asked, 'be equally harmful to your reputation? Wouldn't it be easier to just say "yes"?'

And so, with the chief minister's intervention, all the hurdles were crossed, and preparations for our wedding began.

17

The Jewels in my Crown

On 4 May 1963, a day before my wedding, my baraat left Chandigarh for Pathankot. By now Isher and the rest of my family had accepted the fact that Nimmi and I were going to be married. They arrived for my seharbandi ceremony and took charge of all the rites and rituals. I happily submitted, not having the heart to dampen their enthusiasm. Isher, despite her earlier objections, was elated that her brother had, at last, decided to settle down with the girl of his dreams.

There was almost two hundred of us in my baraat—relatives, colleagues and close friends, among them Kartar Singh and Sardar Umrao Singh, sports minister and president of the Indian Athletics' Association, whom we picked up from Jalandhar.

Thousands of people had congregated on the streets and on the roofs of houses to welcome our cavalcade as we wended our way through the streets and bazaars of Pathankot, cheering and showering us with rose petals. There were loud cries of 'Milkha Singh, Milkha Singh!' When we entered the bride's home, Makhan Singh did the honours, embracing and exchanging garlands with Nimmi's brother, Dev Dutt. Then it was time for the bride's appearance. Supported by her sisters and friends, she slowly came towards me, her head demurely covered by a voluminous dupatta. We garlanded each other. After the jaimala, the reception of the baraat was held, and then my family, friends and I returned to the guesthouse where we were staying.

The next morning, we arrived at the bride's house for the Anand Karaj. Nimmi looked beautiful, all dressed in her wedding finery—a heavy red and gold brocaded sari, her arms covered with bangles dripping with kaliras—as we solemnly circumambulated the sacred Guru Granth Sahib four times, before we were declared man and wife. A lavish lunch followed and then it was time for the vidai, where the bride's family bids their daughter goodbye as she formally enters her husband's home. It was a very long, emotional and tearful farewell before I tenderly put Nimmi into my trusty Fiat and we began our journey back to Chandigarh.

A grand reception was held in Chandigarh the next day before we left for our honeymoon in Srinagar. At the reception, attended by ministers, celebrated sportspeople and other distinguished guests, the chief minister, Kairon Sahib, made a speech in which he showered blessings on us and talked about the importance of genes. He said that this was a union between two illustrious sportspeople—an international sprinter and the captain of the Indian volleyball team—whose progeny would surely follow in their footsteps. He hoped that our children would be inspired by our careers and excel in the world of sports as well. At that stage, I had thought it was too early to predict the future. All that I was aware of was my new bride by my side, and that though I had won many medals, awards and prizes in my career, all these paled before Nimmi, who has remained the brightest, most treasured trophy God has given me.

Our early life together soon settled into some kind of a routine. That we both worked at the same office had its advantages, it made our daily commute much easier and gave us a common ground of interest. We also shared a deep love for sports, and Nimmi always supported and encouraged me, whether it was on the track or when I was setting up projects for the promotion of sports in Punjab. She was a brilliant administrator and I would usually ask her for advice when I was hassled by some technical detail or bureaucratic obstacle.

Our happiness multiplied when Nimmi gave birth to our first daughter in January 1964. It is one of life's most special moments to hold one's first born in one's arms, to watch her smile and gurgle, and to adapt to the joys of parenthood. We named her Aleeza, a name suggested by an English swimming coach who was a close friend of ours. Our second daughter, Mona, arrived in August 1965, followed by another daughter in December 1967. Our third daughter was named Sonia because she was *bahut soni*, so pretty. We were delighted with our daughters, and felt that our family was now complete. But fate had other plans for us, when we discovered that Nimmi was pregnant again. Our fourth child, a son, was born in December 1970. When I gazed down into his eyes, I saw my reflection in them. We named him Chiranjeev Milkha Singh.

Nimmi was a devoted wife and mother. I am still amazed by how efficiently she managed her personal and professional life without letting either of them suffer. She was the perfect housewife, running our home so smoothly that all our needs were taken care of. She ensured that there was always good, hearty food on the table, looked after the children, supervised their homework, and yet, never neglected her official responsibilities. But, we still worried whether as working parents we could give the children the stability they required while they were growing up. Reluctantly, we decided to send Aleeza, Mona, and even Sonia who just three years old, to St Mary's Convent, a boarding school in Kasauli, a hill station a short distance from Chandigarh. Nimmi was so distraught by this separation that every evening she would look up at the lights of Kasauli and cry—she missed her daughters very much. I couldn't bear to see her so upset and after a few months we brought the girls down and enrolled them in Sacred Heart Convent in Chandigarh.

As a family we shared many interests, attending school events, travelling and a passionate love for dogs. My first pet, in 1958, was a dog I named Dolly after an old girlfriend of mine. Since then, our home has always been filled with dogs of almost every breed—Labradors, golden retrievers, poodles and even an apso. The children would take them for long walks, play with them, groom and feed them. They still haven't lost their affection for dogs.

During the summer holidays, I would take the family with me for camps in the mountains. It was a good experience for them to see a different way of life, and also to understand and appreciate my vocation. They would also accompany me when I went on shikar, and we would spend many happy days in the jungle.

In those days there was no taboo against hunting; instead, it was regarded as a manly pastime, governed by strict rules and regulations that controlled the number of animals killed, among other restrictions. It was mandatory for keen shikaris, like me, to acquire permits to hunt in certain specially designated game resorts, like the Meetawalli Block near Haridwar, which was also the regular haunt of the rich and the famous.

My hunting was restricted to birds and animals, including partridge, duck, wild boar and deer, which we would take home for the table, or if we were on an overnight trip, cook over the campfire.

I've only had a couple of big game encounters, once when I shot a leopard. I must admit that this was one of the most frightening experiences of my life. We were at the Kothi resthouse, along the timber trail in Himachal Pradesh, when I spied a spotted animal sitting on a rock. Thinking that it was a spotted deer or chital, I picked up my gun and shot at the animal, which leapt up and disappeared. We tried to search for it, but could find no blood trails, but then, when I peered into a cave below, I saw a pair of bloodshot eyes staring back at me. It was only then that I realized to my horror that the spotted animal was actually a leopard! Fortunately, my reflexes were quick, and I shot it dead.

My next encounter was when I was walking through the jungle and saw, through the trees, a tigress with two cubs. Not wanting to disturb their frolic, I quickly took a step back and slunk away.

18
I Have a Dream

As the children started growing up, we began to think about their future. My early struggles as an athlete were always at the back of my mind, and I didn't want them to enter a field that offered little money and security. Like my father, it was my desire that the children should receive a good education and earn professional degrees, so that they could become doctors or engineers, solid and conservative careers that would reap dividends in the future. The girls were progressing well at school, but Jeev was a cause of some concern.

Right from a very young age, Jeev had started to show a distinct inclination towards sports; more significant was the fact that he was demonstrating a great aptitude for it as well. He was an excellent sprinter as I noticed when I was the chief guest at one of his school's functions—he was studying at St John's School in Chandigarh then. I saw him run so swiftly that he was far ahead of the other boys. The spectators were most impressed and remarked that he would surely break my records one day. When he was studying at Bishop Cotton in Simla, he was the captain of the school's cricket team, and I remember what Kapil Dev's coach, D.P.S. Azad who worked under me, said, 'Sir, if you allow me to train Jeev, I can assure you that he will be a member of Indian cricket team in just a few years.' Then I recalled Kairon Sahib's wise words about genes, and realized how true they were proving to be. Our daughters, too, were competent sportspersons—Sonia was a superb tennis player, while Aleeza and Mona were good swimmers.

Life can often be unexpected. I first developed an interest in golf as late as 1969, but little did I realize how this game would dominate our lives.

A friend of mine in Edmonton had presented me with a golf set, but I had no wish whatsoever to take up the game and carelessly asked him what I should do with it. He insisted that I should keep it and so, the set came back to India with me. For a long time it languished in a forgotten corner of the house, gathering dust. One day, when I was taking my usual run along the golf course, I was stopped by Dharma Vira, then the governor of Punjab, who asked, 'Milkha, why are you running around the course? Come, I'll teach you how to play golf instead.'

'No', I replied emphatically, 'it's an old man's game, and I find it too slow and boring.' He laughed at my dismissal of the game he loved, and retorted, 'Bring your set tomorrow and I will give you lessons.'

The next day, I dusted the grime off my set, went to the golf course and had my first lesson. I have to admit that the game intrigued me, and after that first lesson I was addicted and would rush to the course whenever I had any free time.

When Jeev was little, he would follow me around the course, fascinated by my every move. Day by day his interest grew until it became an obsession. I had no objection to my children dabbling in sports; what I didn't want was for them to take it up as a professional career. They had been brought up in the lap of luxury and I didn't think that they had the disciple and will power to work hard. In sheer desperation, I got him admitted in one of India's most prestigious public schools, Bishop Cotton in Simla. Both Nimmi and Jeev were very upset but I insisted. He spent two years at Bishop Cotton, from 1983 to 1985.

Though we had sent Jeev to boarding school, his passion for golf did not diminish. It was then that I understood that it was destiny that had led my son to golf.

In January 1985, when he had come down for the winter vacations, Jeev participated and won the American Express Golf Tournament at the Delhi Golf Club. He was thirteen years old. After winning the tournament he returned to Bishop Cotton to sit for the Class 7 final examinations. Meanwhile, we had got him admission in a school in Chandigarh, Shivalik Public School, so that he could study as well as play golf. In June, he left for Woodbridge in England for a month-long coaching camp. This was the starting point on his road to fame.

In 1987, when he was fifteen and in Class 9, he participated in the Doug Sanders golf scholarship selections. He won at each stage of the event: first, the India selection held at the Delhi Golf Club, followed by the Asian selection in Melbourne, concluding with the final selection in Aberdeen. Being awarded the Doug Sanders golf scholarship at the Abilene Christian University, in Houston, Texas, meant that Jeev could combine formal education with a sports curriculum.

All this travelling around meant that he was missing classes at school and he still had to complete his education. The Shivalik Public School, however, was most supportive, and arranged extra classes and special tuitions for him. He completed his Class 10 at this school, and then transferred to DAV College, Sector 10, Chandigarh, for the final two years. In 1991 he passed out of DAV College and left for a new life in Houston, Texas.

Jeev's years in the United States were highly successful ones. He played several NCAA (National Collegiate Athletic Association) division tournaments where he represented his university. I was filled with pride when he won the NCAA II Division championship and when his team came first in the Inter-University Golf Championship in 1993. In the same year, he graduated from Abilene Christian University with an associate degree in business administration and returned to India where he turned pro. Thereafter, he won numerous tournaments on the Asian and European tours. He was also the first Indian to qualify for the European Tour. My hopes for my son had exceeded all expectations.

Today, I am glad that Dharma Vira persuaded me to start playing golf, because it was my fascination for the game that lured Jeev to it. His quick aptitude and inherent skill combined with his passion and determination have made him the gifted sportsman that he is. When I accompany Jeev on his tours, whether it is in India, Europe, the US or elsewhere, and walk beside him when he's playing, my knowledge of the game allows me the freedom to offer not only fatherly advice but professional pointers as well. Besides, it is through him that I relive my days of glory. I was on cloud nine when Jeev was given the Arjuna Award (1999) followed by the Padma Shri (2007).

It has been an amazing journey and today, I am a proud husband, father and grandfather. Nimmi and I keep ourselves busy running the Milkha Charitable Trust in Chandigarh, where we provide humanitarian services to the poor and needy, particularly penniless sportspeople and their families. These are causes that are very close to our hearts.

My children have brought me immense happiness, and though Aleeza and Mona live in the United States, we are as close as if they lived next door. Mona is a doctor, fulfilling my wish that my children would have professional careers. I have five grandchildren—Aleeza's daughter Shaina is now twenty-one years old and her son Ishaan is thirteen, Sonia has twins, a boy and a girl, Amaan and Amaanat who are six, Jeev's son Harjai Milkha Singh is the youngest and is just three. Their future lies ahead, and they are content in knowing that both Nimmi and I will always be there for them, loving and supporting them through the passage of life.

19

Once an Athlete, Always an Athlete

Although I had retired from the track in 1964, I was still much in demand on the international circuit, and would be invited to attend events and meets all over the world. I was there in Munich for the 1972 Olympics and witnessed the tragic shooting of eleven members of the Israeli team, in what must be one of the dastardliest acts in the history of sports. With me in Munich was the celebrated American athlete, Jessie Owens, who had won three gold medals at the 1936 Berlin Olympics, where the world saw, for the first time, the power of Hitler's Nazi Germany. Both were events where the very essence of sportsmanship was overshadowed and diminished by politics.

In 1980, I was the only Indian sportsperson to be as chosen by the United Nations to carry a torch for peace throughout the world. Only the best runners from each country were given the privilege to participate in this humanitarian relay. I remember running along the Great Wall of China, and handing the torch over to the presidents of Nigeria and Kenya, as well as to Giani Zail Singh, who was then president of India.

When Delhi hosted the 1982 Asian Games, I had the honour of lighting the torch at the newly constructed Jawaharlal Nehru Stadium. After the ceremony was over, I was taken to the VIP enclosure and given a seat next to Rajiv Gandhi, his wife, Sonia, and her family. His mother and our prime minister, Indira Gandhi, was seated nearby.

We greeted each other cordially, and then Rajiv turned to his father- and brother-in-law and pointing at me, asked them, 'Do you recognize this man?' They looked blank, but when he explained that I had participated in the 1960 Rome Olympics, they exclaimed in excitement: 'Oh, the saint!' and asked for my autograph. During the Games, whenever I would appear from the tunnel that led into the stadium, the spectators would look at my long hair and beard, and cheer wildly, calling me a guru, a mendicant, a saint. It was that image that had remained in their minds for all these years.

I have always had a very close association with the Nehru–Gandhi family. Panditji loved sports and it was because of his influence that Delhi hosted the 1951 Asian Games. His daughter, Indira, would always joke with me about her running days when she was in school in Switzerland, and how she would always come first in the races. In 1982, at the Veterans' Athletic Meet, she came up to the starting line, hitched up her sari and prepared to join the race. Her security guards were shocked, and pleaded with me to escort her back to the seating enclosure. Such are my warm memories of the Gandhi family.

◆

In the thirty years that I worked in the sports department, first as deputy director of sports, and then director of sports and education, I initiated several projects to promote and improve the quality of sports in the state. Among them was the opening of about thirty or forty sports wings attached to schools and colleges in various districts. The objective was to search for talented young players at the village and district levels and encourage them to take up sports as a career.

We sent messages to the principals of all educational institutions asking them to identify young boys and girls who showed promise in the field of sports, be it hockey, football, volleyball, athletics and more. Officials from our department would visit the schools and check what facilities they offered, including playgrounds, gymnasiums, hockey fields and athletic tracks. The next step was to hold trials and select the best, who were then placed in specially-created sports wings, where the government provided them with free tuition, hostel facilities, food, training and equipment like tracksuits and sports kits.

We set up tough practice schedules and hired qualified coaches who could supervise and monitor their progress. In this way, the budding sportspersons would receive training in sports, and at the same time, continue their education.

The process was further refined according to interest and specialization. If a boy or a girl showed potential in a specific field, whether it was gymnastics, hockey, football or athletics, we would send them to specially designated schools or areas where their talents could be further developed, like for example, Hoshiarpur, which specialized in football. There they could also participate in regular competitions and learn that healthy competitiveness went hand-in-hand with the spirit of sportsmanship. Our persistent efforts and zeal were rewarded and we produced several world-class sportspersons, including Ajit Pal Singh and Surjit Singh—both were students of the sports school in Jalandhar and later captained India in hockey; Balbir Singh Jr represented India in hockey; Ajaib Singh was the 400-metre champion and Mahinder Singh Gill, a triple jumper. Many of them participated in national-level games, and when they won they would be offered lucrative jobs by the railways, police, banks, and even corporate houses like Tata.

All my life, I have firmly believed that a strict training programme under the guidance of professional and competent coaches was the key to success, as well as will power and determination. Those were the principles that I stressed upon during the training period; they were, after all, the very mantras that I had lived by in my early years. I also believed that talent must be nurtured from a very young age for it to grow and flourish. If I hadn't received the support and encouragement from the army when I was starting off, would I have reached the heights that I did?

During the summer vacations in May and June, the department held month-long summer camps in picturesque hill stations such as Srinagar, Simla, Manali, among others. We would book a stadium that had all sports facilities, and organize accommodation and make arrangements for food for almost five hundred boys and girls. The camps adhered to a strict schedule, beginning the day with prayers and a roll call. Thereafter, the time was spent on the field. The weather, fortunately, was cool and pleasant, so being outdoors was always invigorating. My role in the camps was to inspire and motivate each and every child and to convince them that the road to fame was not a bed of roses, that only hard work, dedication, will power and discipline would lead them to their destiny. I would tell them about my early life, about the relentless training schedules I had set for myself, about the toil and perseverance, all because of my overpowering desire to succeed in international events. Because I was so obsessed with training, I would oversee the programme to check if the coaches were being as diligent as they should.

I have very fond memories of the summer camps, particularly of the enthusiastic youngsters who never complained or tried to shirk their duties. I also remember with gratitude the help I received from Kashmir's chief minister, Farooq Abdullah, and his father, Sheikh Abdullah, who welcomed me to Srinagar and provided me with all facilities while we were there, and

General Gurbaksh Singh, who kindly allowed me to hold a camp in Shimla's Annadale grounds, said to be the highest cricket ground in the world at that time. None of this would have been possible if I had been an unknown sports official. They knew and respected me, and above all, believed in what I was doing and never hesitated to extend every support to the cause.

Another policy I initiated in the early 1970s was to make the games period compulsory in every school in Punjab. I had learnt, to my horror, that since this period came at the end of the school day, it was the easiest one to bunk. I sent urgent appeals to all principals and physical training instructors throughout the state, telling them emphatically that it was their responsibility to ensure that all students attend this period, if they wanted their schools' sports standards to improve. The purpose of the period was to teach children to play games, to train them, to tell them what the rules were, but if there were no attendees, the entire exercise would become a farce. I emphasized that it was up to the principals or instructors to set examples, and if they were sincere, committed, and above all, strict, the students would be equally dedicated.

Throughout my tenure, the message I repeatedly sent to all institutions and associations was that if we wanted to improve the quality of sports, not only in Punjab but also throughout India, we should all unite and work towards a common goal. But to achieve that goal, each of us should be sincere and dedicated, whether it was the athlete, the coach or the association. Half-hearted measures will not work. I travelled extensively across Punjab to spread my message. Wherever I went, people would come up to me, saying that my son is a good runner, or is keen on football, can you give him a chance? I would then test them and if they were truly talented, I would place them in the relevant sports wing. What drove me was my deep desire to pass on what I knew to young children. For that purpose, I have never rested in my mission.

Sadly, after I retired, most of my initiatives faded away—no camps have been held since 1991, students continue to bunk the games period, and the standards of the sports wings have deteriorated. The stark truth is that nobody cares or is interested, or has the vision to plan ahead or think of the future of sports in India. It is only by grooming children when they are young that we can create a strong group of sportspeople who will shine in international events. We are such a large and diverse nation, and yet after Milkha Singh and P.T. Usha, there has been no other athlete who has been able to compete successfully in either the Asian or Olympic games.

Just before I retired in 1991, I had sent a request for the Chandigarh government to give me ten acres of land to establish a national-level athletic academy to train and develop young sportspeople. My dream was to build hostels, stadiums and swimming pools, create spaces for athlete tracks, football and hockey fields, and every other facility that such an institution demands. But the idea was summarily dismissed even before it could be discussed or debated impartially. One of the objections put forth was the money required for such a project; the land itself would cost crores of rupees. I was very disillusioned that there was no one who was decisive enough to take a decision, and so a project that was dearest to my heart faded away into oblivion, just like all my other initiatives.

◆

Almost six decades after my first race in 1953, I have come to the sad conclusion that the decline of sports is also because, somewhere over the years, Indian athletes have lost the killer instinct when it comes to winning events at the international level. When I was in China for the 2008 Olympics, I visited several of their sports academies and was impressed by how organized they were and the single-minded determination with which they went about achieving their targets. Their eventual ambition is to become the top sporting nation in the world.

In China, children are selected at a very young age and they train year after year. Talented young athletes are required to undergo a strict training regime, so much so that a gymnast is made to repeat an exercise not once but a million times, until they perfect their technique. Their coaches are equally resolute because they know that they are entirely responsible for their trainees' success or failure. And since failure is not an option, all their energies are concentrated towards ensuring that their students win.

How very different this systematic approach is from the lackadaisical manner in which we try to develop our sportspeople. Selections in India are ad hoc, often dictated by political diktats, or through personal contacts and connections. What India needs today is a firm goal to aspire towards, and what could be more prestigious than aiming for an Olympic gold? Success in the Olympics should be our ambition, but to achieve that end, we need international-level coaching, and for that, I would strongly recommend emulating the Chinese, right from creating a world-class sports infrastructure to spotting and grooming kids with talent. We need to overhaul our selection process and training methodology and choose only the most talented young boys and girls who show promise and have the potential to produce results. Give them professional guidance, use scientific training methods, discipline them if their standards fall, and above all, inspire and motivate them. What needs to be instilled in them right from the beginning is: toil hard to increase efficiency, stamina and strength, be resolute in thought, word and deed, and most important of all, take pride in your performance.

But no sportsperson can achieve results without an equally dedicated and committed coach. Thousands of coaches graduate from the National Institute of Sports (NIS) every year, but what has been their contribution to the development of our sportspeople? Unlike China, they are not held accountable if their trainees do not produce the expected results. The sad truth is that no one questions them, neither the government who employs them, nor the associations who sponsor them, not even their students whose careers depend upon them. As a result, they have grown complacent in their jobs.

A lethargic or apathetic coach can only impede the growth and progress of an athlete. If there were no Gurdev Singh, Ranbir Singh or Dr Howard when I first started running, would I have ever achieved the success I did? No. And I will reiterate what I have always said that it is only the coach who has the power and influence to build a sportsperson's stamina, prowess and self-confidence.

To rid ourselves of this malaise, I would suggest that the government should not employ coaches on a permanent basis, simply because as government employees they have the security, if not job satisfaction, and when they retire they are assured of their pensions. India desperately needs more coaches like Pullela Gopichand, whose student, the world-class badminton champion Saina Nehwal, is a credit to his patience and meticulous grooming. And, if we are really serious about wanting to improve the situation, we need to be more careful about our selection of coaches: hire those who are capable and who share the same goals, give them four-year contracts on the assurance that their contracts will be renewed only after they have produced some tangible results. They must be made to understand that during this period their performance will be judged by how they and their students perform. The performers would then be rewarded, while the non-performers should be shown the door. Every country hires coaches on a contract basis, so why not India? But such a change will only be possible once the current group of coaches retires, and government and sports associations are ready to take on a new challenge.

20

The Politics of Sports

It is common knowledge that the international sports calendar is fixed years in advance to give every participating nation the opportunity to prepare for them, whether it is to train athletes or for the host country to set up the required infrastructure. The New Delhi Commonwealth Games 2010 was not the best example of either.

India's hosting of this sporting extravaganza led to an unfortunate chain of events, starting with charges of large-scale corruption in the organization of the Commonwealth Games against certain people, who were subsequently jailed because of these charges, and eventually ending in the International

Olympic Committee (IOC) suspending the Indian Olympic Association in December 2012. What this means is that unless India is readmitted by the IOC, no Indian athlete can compete at future Olympic Games.

For sports to flourish in India, drastic measures need to be urgently taken. There has to be a unanimous agreement between the government, sports federations and associations, to discard personal agendas and gains and strive towards a common goal. The government has provided more than adequate funds and several state-of-the-art facilities, but what are they getting in return? Hard-hitting questions need to be asked: what are the plans for the future? What has been done to implement them? Have funds been honestly disbursed? It is only when these questions have been debated and answered should funds be allocated.

Many initiatives can be taken if we want standards to improve. But, first there must be a desire to change the system. Our one-point agenda should be to groom sportspeople to succeed in national and international events, to win medals and accolades. A strategic plan needs to be put in place and implemented decisively and purposefully. One way could be to identify areas where talent exists and tap it—for example, wrestling in Haryana, archery in the Northeast, hockey in Punjab. Planning must be focused and enforced honestly—only then can India emerge as a front liner in the sports world. Each one of us must contribute if we want to change the system.

The all-pervading influence of politics on sports has to end. A while ago, the sports ministry had invited me to sit on the board of the Athletic Federation; I attended some meetings, but soon realized that I was in the minority, and that my frank views were not welcome. Several people with vested interests resented my presence on the board, only because they felt that a veteran athlete like myself would eclipse their prominence. Often I used to wonder how people who have never played a game could have been given such important positions. Why couldn't sportspeople head sports organizations? But this can never happen, simply because vested interests will prevent such a move. More important is the fact that these are elected positions and no sportsman will be able to garner more votes than a wily and powerful politician.

When Margaret Alva was the sports minister, I often told her that all heads of influential sports bodies should have tenures of just five years, so that there will be a change in the style of functioning. I voiced the same opinion to the next minister, Ajay Maken, but only an act of Parliament can initiate such a policy.

What we can't comprehend is that the world is changing rapidly and that we will be left far, far behind if we don't move with the times. In all these decades, sports technology, too, has changed. When I was starting my career in the early 1950s, there were no running shoes, and it was only in 1956 after Roshan Sports in Patiala began to manufacture them, that they were accessible to the public. Another revolutionary change has been the introduction of synthetic tracks. This has meant that athletes have achieved feats that were considered near impossible during our times. With shoes, tracksuits and other sophisticated equipment and benefits so readily and openly available, why then is it so difficult for our sportspeople to reach international standards?

What saddens me most today is the universal use of drugs. When I used to run, the only drugs I knew of were those taken for medicinal purposes, yet today, drugs have spread like cancer, even at the school games' competition levels. Visit any educational institution in the Punjab, and you will find needles and other substance abuse paraphernalia lying around openly. Drugs are easily available either in medical stores or through dealers, and each person, whether a child or adult, knows what drug to take, when and how much. Up-and-coming young athletes have no qualms about taking any type of illegal substances, whether it is heroin, cocaine, or banned supplement drugs to enhance their performances to achieve spectacular results without hard work. The authorities are aware of what is taking place, so are the coaches and doctors who pretend that they don't. In the last few years, there has been a spate of scandals regarding the use of drugs among Indian sportspeople.

Two members of the Indian women's 4x400-metre relay team who won gold medals at the Delhi Commonwealth Games in 2010, later tested positive for the use of performance-enhancing steroids; more recently was the unexpected allegation that Olympic bronze-medallist, Vijender Singh, had taken heroin and other banned substances, though the tests turned out to be negative. Despite the personal humiliation and disgrace of medals being returned and dishonour to the country, no action has been taken to stop the spread of drugs. If the government and sports authorities are serious about the eradication of illegal drugs, they must act swiftly and enforce a strict clampdown on all the sources and suppliers; ban athletes who take drugs from participating in future events, and suspend or sack doctors and coaches who are responsible for importing drugs or introducing them to their students. Strong, almost authoritarian, measures are the only ways in which to deal with such serious and harmful practices.

◆

In 2001, the Bharatiya Janata Party government offered me the Arjuna Award, almost forty years after I had received the more prestigious Padma Shri in 1958. When the award was introduced in 1961, its premise was very clear—that it would only be granted to those outstanding sportspeople who had received medals in international events, including the Olympic, Asian and Commonwealth games.

When I looked at the list I discovered that it included even team members for games which have no global presence like kabbadi, which is played in just four countries. I brought this and other examples of unworthy candidates to the notice of the then minister of sports, Uma Bharati, and told her that I considered it a farce to be included in the same list of nominees who have not even represented their country. It was as if the Arjunas had been given away like prasad, to any and everybody, ignoring those who truly deserve them.

I firmly refused the award because the selection committee had ignored the fundamental premise on which it was founded, and that by giving me the award at this stage it did not recognize 'the stature of the services I had rendered to the nation'. If her government had wanted to give me an award, why didn't they separate my name from the general list, and announce that they were honouring me with a lifetime achievement award? Moreover, why has it taken so long for my achievements to be acknowledged and recognized? After all, I had received a Padma Shri at the height of my career, when I was 'Asia's Best Athlete' and the 'Nation's Pride'. My refusal made headline news, but as far as I was concerned, if the government had wanted to offer me an Arjuna, why did it take them forty years?

Besides the Padma Shri, my other awards included the Helms World Trophy for the best athlete in the world presented by the United States of America in 1959, and the Indira Priyadarshini Gandhi Award in 1997. Such awards and decorations play a major role in boosting a sportsman's morale, they bring fame and immortalize a person's name, but unfortunately very few of them bring great financial benefits. In the early years of the Arjuna Award, sportspeople received a sum of money, but few benefits, unlike today when awardees are entitled to railway passes, discounted airfares, petrol and gas agencies, among others.

I have always been a strong advocate for the cause of continuing official patronage for prominent sportspeople when they retire. Most sportspeople come from indigent, uneducated backgrounds, whose parents neither had the means nor the influence to develop their child's potential. But what differentiated these children from the rest was their hunger and drive to develop their abilities and succeed.

But what happens when they retire? They have no family

money or assets to fall back on, and their brief careers have not provided them with a secure future; they receive no benefits or any monetary gain, and once they leave the field, they are forgotten. There have been so many tragic stories of sportspeople, even Arjuna awardees and gold medallists, who have died in abject poverty, including Dhyan Chand and Trilok Singh. I have often suggested to the government that they should introduce some schemes that will help sportspeople when they retire—give them jobs, a regular pension and other benefits. The more prominent ones can be appointed to sports bodies, or even as state governors. Such incentives will encourage the aspiring youth to choose sports as a career.

Another reason why sports standards are declining is that over the last few decades, cricket has overshadowed every other sport in India. Open any newspaper, put on the television, and what first grabs a person's attention are the screaming headlines and images of star cricketers in action. No other sport gets the kind of exaggerated coverage that cricket does. Besides, there's a constant cycle of cricket—test matches, one-dayers, IPL and what not—taking place throughout the year, so many events that there seems to be very little respite between one match and the next. Compelling images, swashbuckling exploits, glamorous lifestyles, and most important, the money are the lures that attract young children towards the game.

Just a handful of youngsters are interested in any other sport. Even if a sportsperson wins or breaks a record in any other game, be it athletics, hockey, boxing, wrestling, shooting, tennis or badminton, attention will focus on them for only a short while. For example, our medallists at the 2012 London Olympics, including Saina Nehwal, Sushil Kumar, M.C. Mary Kom, were greatly fêted for their successes when they returned, but then the attention was back to cricket once again. I think the media should help encourage other sports in every possible way.

A vital ingredient to promote a product, a film, a book or a sport is publicity, which is why cricket has become such a dominant sport today. When my first autobiography was released in Punjabi in the mid-1970s, I had hundreds of fans, children and adults alike, coming up to me, saying that they wanted to be Milkha Singh. I would then put them in the training programme, but after four or five days they would abscond because they could not cope with the gruelling routine. I would ask, 'Do you think that to become Milkha Singh is a joke? A sleight of hand? No, to be Milkha Singh, you need courage and conviction, as well a goal to aspire towards.' And for me, that goal always was to excel in running. Otherwise, would I have practised so relentlessly?

◆

Some years ago, I donated my medals, trophies and other sports memorabilia to the NIS, Patiala, and Delhi's National Stadium, while the spiked shoes I wore to run the 1960 Rome Olympics was donated by me for a charity auction organized by actor Rahul Bose's NGO, The Foundation. Rakeysh Omprakash Mehra, who made the film on my early life and running days—*Bhaag Milkha Bhaag*—bought the shoes for twenty-four lakh rupees.

Life has given me much more than I hoped for, however,

I have one remaining desire: to see an Indian runner win back the Olympic medal that slipped away from my hand on that fateful day in Rome.

Epilogue

I am neither a writer nor an author, but a sportsman with passion who has poured his heart out in this book. Although I am not a man of words, I hope this book can inspire the youth to take up sports and strive to excel.

I am proud of the fact I am a self-made man. My philosophy is very simple: 'The lines on our palms do not decide our future, *kambakht*, we, too, have a say in it.' Hard work can change destiny as I know only too well—my entire life has been dedicated to it. My early years were a struggle, but as I gradually started to achieve results, my name and fame grew. I won competitions and medals, except for the elusive Olympic gold, which I will always regret, and yet I have always been content because I kept trying.

My final words would be: life as a sportsperson is hard, and there will certainly be times when you might be tempted to quit, or take shortcuts—but remember there are no shortcuts to success. At such times you should try and derive inspiration from this Urdu couplet:

Mita de apni hasti ko agar koi martaba chahe,
ki dana khak may mil kar gul-e-gulzar hota hai

Destroy your entire existence if you want to reach the zenith,
'Cos a seed has to become one with the dust to sprout and blossom into a flower.